**The Last Mask**

T0079763

Brian Alkire

**The Last Mask**
**Hamann's Theater of the Grotesque**

DIAPHANES

**THINK ART** Series of the Institute for Critical Theory (ith)—
Zurich University of the Arts and the Centre for Arts and
Cultural Theory (ZKK)—University of Zurich.

Made possible with the generous support of the Centre for Arts and
Cultural Theory (ZKK), the Department of Comparative Literature (AVL),
and the *Forschungskredit* of the University of Zurich (Grant No. FK-19-057).

© DIAPHANES, Zurich 2021
All rights reserved

ISBN 978-3-0358-0370-9

Cover image: *Mask of Papposilenus*, Bronze, h. 38.7 cm
First half of 1st century BC.
© Fondazione Sorgente Group, Rome

Layout: 2edit, Zurich
Printed in Germany

www.diaphanes.com

# Table of Contents

If you want to be a learned conqueror like Bacchus then you would do well to choose a Silenus for your companion. I do not love wine for wine's sake but because it gives me a tongue to tell you the truth in my stupor on the back of my donkey.
—Hamann to Kant, late December 1759

The mask, the costume, the covered is everywhere the truth of the uncovered. The mask is the true subject of repetition. Because repetition differs in kind from representation, the repeated cannot be represented: rather, it must always be signified, masked by what signifies it, itself masking what it signifies...
—Gilles Deleuze, *Difference and Repetition*

## Abbreviations of Cited Hamann Editions

R:   Johann Georg Hamann, *Fliegender Brief: Historisch-kritische Ausgabe mit einer Einführung, Kommentar und Dokumenten zur Entstehungs-geschichte,* ed. Janina Reibold, 2 vols. (Hamburg: Felix Meiner Verlag, 2018). Cited by sheet number.

W:   Reiner Wild, *"Metacriticus bonae spei": Johann Georg Hamanns "Flie-gender Brief," Einführung, Text und Kommentar* (Bern and Frankfurt: Herbert Lang/Peter Lang, 1975).

N:   Johann Georg Hamann, *Sämtliche Werke,* ed. Josef Nadler, 6 vols. (Vienna: Verlag Herder, 1949–1957).

ZH:  Johann Georg Hamann, *Briefwechsel,* ed. Walther Ziesemer (vols. 1–3) and Arthur Henkel (vols. 1–7), 7 vols. (Wiesbaden and Frankfurt: Insel Verlag, 1955–1979). Cited according to letter number. Ongoing digiti-zation at hamann-briefe.de.

# 1. Theory in Theater: Hamann's Metacritical Masquerade

What *was* Hamann?—From the first pages of his first published work, *Socratic Memorabilia* (1759), where he announces his decision to "condescend to borrow the veil woven by a patriotic St. John and a Platonic Shaftesbury for their unbelief and misbelief" (N II 61), to the failure and abandonment of his final work and planned unmasking *Disrobing and Transfiguration* (1786), Johann Georg Hamann remained consistent on one point at least: he is communicating to us through a series of veils, masks, personae, and disguises stitched together[1] from the words of others, from the language of his contemporaries and from the depths of his vast body of reading. These hyperreferential mosaic[2] masks are tessellated to fit particular occasions, usually combative and antagonistic reactions to contemporaries, to friends as well as enemies (or in the case of Kant, Herder, and Mendelssohn, the enemy *in* the friend), to books, translations, reviews, and contemporary political developments. As he bluntly put it to his friend and correspondent Friedrich Jacobi (1743–1819) in a letter near

---

1 The Greek verb *rhapsoidein* ("to stitch songs together") referred to the recitation of selected patches of Homer stitched together into a single recitation session. Plato in *Ion* called the rhapsode the interpreter of the interpreter. Shaftesbury used the term *Philosophical Rhapsody* to refer to his mode of essay-writing. Hamann adopts the term for his own style, most famously in the subtitle of "*Aesthetica in nuce*: A Rhapsody in Cabbalistic Prose" (1762).

2 A central term both for Hamann and in Hamann scholarship. His 1762 collection of works in French, for example, was titled *Essais à la mosaïque* (N II 277–297). Also see his reference to François Hemsterhuis' comments about works of mosaic with "ambiguous [*equivoque*] contours" below, p. 71–72.

the end of his life: "The entire fable of my authorship is also a mask."[3]

This element of masquerade—with the inevitable questions it raises concerning truth, reality, ambiguity, and authenticity, the *actual* voice or face behind the mask—is perhaps the greatest challenge in reading a Hamann text, more than the often laborious process of looking up all the references or the perils of getting lost in ever remoter intertextual fields, both of which are becoming easier every year with the advance of search engines, library digitization, and machine translation.[4] This intertextual labor—identifying, sourcing, and reading the referenced intertexts—tends in fact to generate *more* rather than less ambiguity, to bring us farther away from what we thought we were reading in the first place.

Goethe, Hamann's most fruitful reader, wrote in his autobiography of a sensation of irresolvable doubleness upon *returning* to a Hamann text:

> In my collection there are several of his printed proofs where, in
> his own hand, he has cited the passages to which his allusions
> refer. If you look them up, there is once again this ambiguous
> [*zweideutiges*] double light which appears to us extremely pleas-
> ing; the only thing is that you have to entirely give up what is

3    February 25, 1786 (ZH 936).
4    Any discussion about Hamann's obscurity needs to take into account the radical change in reading practices made possible in the past several years, at least insofar as it concerns erudition, memory, and access to documents. This is particularly true in the German-speaking world, where the intense digitization efforts of libraries, archives, and universities have made virtually all texts Hamann references available, often in facsimile first editions. It is now possible to look at the same editions Hamann cites, and even follow specific page references. Hamann is easier to read today than ever, and will only become more readable with time.

> normally called understanding. ... Every time you open them up
> you expect to find something new, because the sense dwelling in
> every passage touches and excites us in manifold ways.[5]

This glimmering doubleness is not a simple side-effect or ob-
stacle to be overcome in the quest for a supposed underlying
univocal meaning. Hamann systematically refuses to provide
routes out of this suspense. He in fact seeks to intensify it as
an explicit act of aggression, a "holy maledictory apostrophe"
(*heilige Verwünschungsapostrophe*) (ZH 936) directed at the
reader and public. This has led to a broad range of reactions
over the course of his reception—and it is hard not to have
a reaction, as Hamann trades in affects: whether repulsion,
disdain, and outrage (e.g. of Enlightenment book reviewers
in Berlin), frustration and anxiety (e.g. Hegel: the herme-
neutic urge to resolve this anxiety[6]), or fascination, pleasure,
and amazement, as with Goethe. This sense of fascination is
rooted in an experience somehow *optical* ("appears," "double
light," "look at") and *kinesthetic* (looking up, opening up,
dwelling in). Hamann's texts emerge as three-dimensional
reflective surfaces with an ability to continually generate new
meanings and sensations, to be different at every encounter.

For Goethe, Hamann's texts are things to be *beheld* rather
than *read*. He is not alone in this response: Hamann's contemporary Moses Mendelssohn, for example, while coming to
the opposite conclusion about the worth of this style, also uses
this kind of kinesthetic and optical language:

---

5    Johann Wolfgang von Goethe, *Goethes Werke: Hamburger Ausgabe in
14 Bänden*, Band 10, ed. Erich Trunz (Hamburg: Christian Wegner, 1948),
p. 514. Unless otherwise noted, all translations in the following are mine.
6    Georg Wilhelm Friedrich Hegel, "Hamann's Schriften," *Werke*, vol. 11,
ed. Eva Moldenhauer and Karl Markus Michel (Frankfurt: Suhrkamp, 1986),
p. 275–389.

One is willing to put up with journeying through the dismal false tracks [*Irrwege*] of an underground cave if one can learn sublime and important secrets at the end; but if one can expect nothing more than *whims* as a reward, then the writer is going to remain unread.[7]

Hamann himself repeatedly uses similar language to describe his and/or the sculptor Socrates' "plastic" style,[8] writes of the "acts" and "closing scenes" (W 306) of his works, of their "dramatic knot[s]" (ZH 913) instead e.g. of arguments, sections, or chapters. These are ideas which thread their way through Hamann's body of work and relate to core questions concerning simultaneity and presence (and their doubles, sequence and absence) in language and writing—which is ultimately, for Hamann, a matter of interrogating the *substance* of language itself.

Comparing the reactions of Goethe and Mendelssohn might provide us with some clues about how to read Hamann, what *kinds* of texts he was writing. Both use the language of *optics* and *embodied experience* to emphasize opposite *effects*: Goethe sees light and experiences fascination, the pleasures of ambiguity, while Mendelssohn emphasizes darkness, error, and labor, expecting a tangible reward, resolution, or discursive proposition at the end of the process. Hamann's texts are, of course, designed to provoke such a search for secrets or mysteries, often to an almost ludicrous degree—this is, after all, the inventor of titles as alluring as "A Rhapsody in Cabbalistic

7    As cited by Hegel in "Hamann's Schriften," p. 332.
8    With Socrates' background as sculptor in mind, *plasticity* of style also stands at the beginning and end of Hamann's work. In *Socratic Memorabilia* we read that "Socrates' writing style would have been more plastic than painterly" (N II 80); in *Disrobing and Transfiguration* Hamann calls it his "exotic plasticity" (R 5, 5r).

Prose" (1762) or "The Last Will and Testament of the Knight of the Rose-Cross" (1772), a writer whose vocabulary suggests an intimate knowledge of alchemy in its actual practice, the possession of actual serious secrets.

To behold, look, perceive: θεάομαι (*theaomai*) in Greek, the shared root of θέα (*thea*), θεωρία (*theoria*) and θέατρον (*theatron*), sight, theory, and theater,[9] and in turn of the sense of "amazement" or "wonder" (θαῦμα, *thauma*) at the origins of philosophy in Aristotle's *Metaphysics*[10] as well as two important religious events in Athens: the Eleusinian mysteries and the Olympic games.[11] This is a form of perception related to but distinct from αἴσθησις (*aisthesis*), perception through the concrete organs of perception, the multiple senses—like taste. *Theoria* and *theatron*, theory and theater, are inherently *double*,[12] delimited spheres of elevated attention, while *aisthesis* is either unitary (sensual perception as such) or multiform (in the various senses). Hamann, who expressed mocking disdain for the science of "aesthetics" which had emerged in his lifetime,[13] also brings a highly—often extravagantly—body- and sense-rooted approach to both aesthetics and theory, although here, as everywhere else, he makes a choice for the totally equivocal, undecidable *double*—suggesting that the single and the multiple somehow irresistibly resolve into each

9    See Dieter Mersch, Sylvia Sasse, and Sandro Zanetti, eds., *Aesthetic Theory*, trans. Brian Alkire (Zurich: diaphanes, 2019), particularly the introduction and Dieter Mersch's contribution (p. 219–236).
10    *Metaphysics*, 982b.
11    Pausanias, *Description of Greece*, 5.10.1.
12    See also: Marco Baschera, *Das Zeichen und sein Double*, ed. Monika Kasper and Christian Villiger (Würzburg: Königshausen und Neumann, 2017).
13    W 324: "With blinking readers who look at writers as peripatetic trees, I must speak in their own aesthetic language which they gave to me [*in ihrer eigenen mir gegebenen ästhetischen Sprache*]."

other: namely into *sensus communis*, the sense of the senses or common sense.

In his final project, *Disrobing and Transfiguration: A Flying Letter to Nobody, the Well-known* (referred to from here as the *Letter*), he brings a new word and concept into play, one which had previously been restricted to the realm of theology, primarily concerning the Eucharist and the "Real Presence" of Christ within it: *virtuality*. In the *Letter,* Hamann outlines a theory of the virtual which is, at the same time, a *virtual theory*—not the *either/or* of his most loyal reader Kierkegaard, nor just a form of experimental philosophy in imitation of the natural scientist[14] but rather the generation of an irresolvable and (hence) productive *yes-and-no*. It is a theory of *observation* (which "*disrobes* actual objects into naked concepts and merely thinkable characteristics, into pure appearances and phenomena"), *fiction* (which "*transfigures* visions of absent past and future into present representations [*Darstellungen*]"), and *criticism* (which "*resists* the usurpations of both powers") (W 334, emphases mine) and the role in all three of the virtual, the yes-and-no, the dynamics of presence, absence, and effect.

Criticism for Hamann is a *double resistance*, not a reconciliation, combination, or transcendence. This resistance takes place through incorporation, a kind of cannibalization: gathering words, images, ideas, and figures and pouring them into a grotesque, ambivalent *ragoût*, a witches' brew both re-

14    In *Socratic Memorabilia*, Hamann drops one of his highly quotable aphorisms: "A diligent interpreter must imitate the natural scientist [*Naturforscher*]" (N II 71). Taking this as a sound basis for how Hamann conceives of his project is to too-hastily assign Hamann the role of interpreter, for which I see relatively little evidence: Hamann seems mainly concerned with how *he* should be interpreted. Cf. the passage in the *Letter* below (p. 65), where the critic's role is precisely *not* interpretation but "simply skillfulness in correctly reciting what he has read" (W 302).

pulsive and intriguing, of different languages, genres, voices, eras, vocabularies, etc. Not a soup but a stew: in the same pot but phasally different, heterogeneous elements brought into internal confrontation and self-collision, chunks of *this* colliding with cuttings of *that* in a broth of *the other thing*, bubbling, steaming, mingling, roiling around—*saturating*.[15]

Many scholars and commentators over the last two centuries have been tempted to resolve the doubleness and evasiveness of Hamann's critical persona into reliable, univocal propositional statements and thus a reliably univocal "Hamann." These readings often crystallize around one or two favorite well-known aphoristic dictums along the lines of "reason is language, *logos*," (ZH 177) "poetry is the mother tongue of the human race," (N II 197) "theology is grammar,"[16] "syllables and letters are pure forms a priori,"[17] etc. Hamann, through his peculiar sort of textual alchemy, seems to have prefigured everyone following him—here he's a forerunner of the linguistic turn and deconstruction, there a radical empiricist who calls for philology to behave like a natural science; here he's an enraged enemy of Enlightenment, there a "radical

---

15   From Athenaeus' banquets to Wagner's comical *ragoûts* in Goethe's *Faust*, satire has always had a connection to food, cooking, and eating, a rhetorical history explored by Sina Dell'Anno in "Fragmente einer Poetik des saturierten Texts," in *Unverfügbares Verinnerlichen: Figuren der Einverleibung zwischen Eucharistie und Anthropophagie*, ed. Yvonne Al-Taie and Marta Famula (Leiden and Boston: Brill/Rodolpi, 2021), p. 89–112.

16   In a 1760 essay on the relationship between money and language called "Mixed Remarks on Word Order in the French Language" (N II 129). One of the best studies of Hamann yet written focuses on this short text: Erich Achermann, *Worte und Werte: Geld und Sprache bei Gottfried Wilhelm Leibniz, Johann Georg Hamann und Adam Müller* (Tübingen: Max Niemeyer, 1997), p. 150–256. Achermann also briefly touches on the *Letter* and Hamann's "Panische Styl" on p. 156, note 32.

17   In "Metacritique on the Purism of Reason" (N III 286).

enlightener"[18] from within, if on the margins; we find him in the notebooks of Wittgenstein,[19] on the desk of Hegel, Benjamin likening his entire project to Hamann's,[20] we see Goethe planning to personally edit his collected works, and then— strange!—Goethe and Hegel meeting for the first and only time and spending the entire evening speaking of Hamann, a youthful passion of both. There he is in the pages of Kierkegaard, Nietzsche, Celan, and so on. Hamann is everywhere and yet, somehow, nowhere—like the public to whom his first and last works are dedicated: *Niemand den Kundbaren,* the no one we all know.[21]

## Satire and the cult of error

The problem with reading Hamann discursively is that there *cannot* be any unequivocal propositional content (statements, *Aussagen*) in a Hamann text: these texts are in a fundamental, self-conscious, and fully emphatic way *pure error*, nothing *but* error, even an assertion that all human thought, language, and action can by nature be nothing but error, *Irrthum*. He

18   Oswald Bayer, *A Contemporary in Dissent: Johann Georg Hamann as Radical Enlightener*, trans. Roy A. Harrisville and Mark C. Mattes (Grand Rapids, Mich. and Cambridge, UK: William B. Eerdmans, 2012).
19   See Lauri Juhana Olavinpoika Snellman, "Hamann's Influence on Wittgenstein," *Nordic Wittgenstein Review* 7/1 (2018): p. 59–82.
20   Walter Benjamin, *Selected Writings*, vol. 1, ed. Howard Eiland and Michael W. Jennings (Cambridge, Mass. and London: Harvard University Press, 1991–1999), p. 107–108.
21   For more on the intricacies of "Nobody the Well-known" and Hamann's dedications, see Andrea Krauss, "Hamann's Latent Parrhesia: Intertextual Exploration of the Self in *Sokratische Denkwürdigkeiten*," in *Self-Reflection in Literature*, eds. Florian Lippert and Marcel Schmidt (Leiden and Boston: Brill/Rodopi, 2019), p. 55–80, here p. 62–65.

expresses this from the beginning: "Some truths," he writes in a letter to his friend Johann Gotthelf Lindner (1729–1776) after finishing *Socratic Memorabilia*, "can only be expressed in a very contrary spirit" (ZH 160). The problem lies in the at first glance innocuous words *some* and *very*: which truths? *How* contrary a spirit? Hamann never lets us know, because he never himself figured it out, nor could, nor wanted to.

This cult of error (the mistake, the falsehood, the lie, the deception) is central to Hamann's literary project and self-understanding, both publicly as a writer and privately, the latter brought to a remarkable point in an account written by Princess Amalia von Gallitzin (1748–1806) shortly after his unexpected death after a stay in her home in Münster in 1788. Hamann's health had been rapidly declining and he was eager to leave Münster and return to Düsseldorf where his friend Jacobi was waiting. His son, Johann Michael, wanted to prevent him from taking the trip, telling him that it would be a grave "error" which could only end in his death. Hamann, in von Gallitzin's account, "finally replied, somewhat reluctantly, 'Son, you know better than anyone else that *errare humanum est*.'"[22] This seems to have impacted Princess Amalia quite deeply, as it triggered her to recall Hamann's comments about his own compulsion to argue whatever he sensed was the opposite of his interlocutor's position; it also caused this recent convert to Roman Catholicism to adopt the distinctively Protestant doctrine of the total depravity of all human acts. This personal and literary cult of error and depravity, with its roots in Humanist and Reformation thought and literature of the

---

22    The account is appended to a 19th century collection of Hamann's writing: Johann Georg Hamann, *Johann Georg Hamann's Schriften und Briefe in vier Teilen*, vierter Teil, ed. Moritz Petri (Hanover: Carl Meyer, 1874), p. 545.

15th to 18th centuries, helps us situate Hamann in an intellectual and literary history, and not just in theology or philosophy but alongside figures like his compulsively-referenced Don Quixote and, even more acutely, Goethe's Faust—*Heinrich Faust*[23]—and his cult of error redeemed through striving.

By examining more *distantly* not only the explicit intertextual references inscribed in the published texts but also the trans- or metatextual references he consistently employs when articulating his self-understanding as a writer,[24] we see a distinct and surprisingly little addressed[25] authorial persona emerge. Hamann's literary models are, almost without exception, writers of *satire*, especially satire in the Menippean mode of Lucian, Apuleius, Ariosto, Rabelais, Johann Fischart, Cervantes, Sterne, as well as a number of writers in the 17th and 18th century English critical tradition (Dryden, Butler,

23   Arnd Böhm raises the not-unlikely prospect that Faust may have been renamed with Hamann in mind: Goethe's Faust was named Heinrich: the historical-legendary Faust was named Johann Georg Faust. See Arnd Böhm, "Naming Goethe's Faust: A Matter of Significance," *Deutsche Vierteljahrsschrift für Literaturwissenschaft und Geistesgeschichte* 80/3 (2006): p. 408–434.

24   Particularly in titles, mottos, and epigraphs, a point which will be explicitly addressed in the *Letter*. Persius in *Socratic Memorabilia* and the *Prolegomena* (N III 123–133), Horace in *Writers and Critics* (*Schriftsteller und Kunstricher*, N III 329–338), Cervantes and Plautus in *Some Things and Something* (*Mancherley, und Etwas*, 1774), Ariosto in *Doubts and Whims* (*Zweifel und Einfälle*, 1776), Apuleius in *Konxompax* (1779), etc.

25   The only two Hamann scholars I have encountered who approach Hamann not just as a writer who *sometimes* employs the tools of satire and parody but as a writer only fully comprehensible *as* a satir*ist* are Dell'Anno and Andre Rudolph. See Andre Rudolph, *"Satiriker unter sich: Lichtenberg – Nicolai – Hamann," Lichtenberg-Jahrbuch 2006*, ed. Ulrich Joost et al. (Saarbrücken: SDV, 2006), p. 86–100, and Dell'Anno, "Fragmente". I only became aware of Dell'Anno's work right as this book was going to press, but am delighted to see that we arrived independently at a number of similar conclusions.

Johnson, Addison, Shaftesbury, Richard Hurd). Two of the most frequently mentioned and defining of these are Rabelais and Cervantes. The former is the ostentatiously hypererudite (and often just as cryptic, referential, and citational) master of the literary *grotesque*, the *carnival* on the page;[26] the latter the chronicler of the dangers and redemptions of obsessed readers, of selves composed of texts, of the nature of masks, performance, and playacting—and the stakes of *performing to ourselves, for ourselves*, the risks and horizons of believing what we are telling ourselves.

Hamann's masks are rarely if ever the somber, mystical veils of Moses speaking the words of Yahweh, or Socrates by the river in Plato's *Phaedrus*, but instead the ambiguous and cryptic mask of Silenus, teacher of Bacchus, companion of Pan and the satyrs, donkey-riding patron of drunken mad holy fools (who sometimes, if you trick them, speak sense), of satyr-plays and satire and tragicomedy (or is it comitragedy?), of Rabelais, Fischart, Cervantes, and Sterne.

The insinuation, with varying degrees of coyness, playfulness, and subtlety, of the presence of secret or hidden meanings behind the pageant of ludicrous or grotesque figures and scenes is a central feature of this mode of satire. Silenus and the sileni boxes named after him make a famous appearance in the prologue of Rabelais' *Gargantua* (1535), igniting half a millennium of debate about the "hidden" meaning of the work:

> Most shining of drinkers, and you, most be-carbuncled of syphilitics – for my writings are addressed solely to you – Alcibiades, praising in a dialogue of Plato's called *The Banquet* his teacher

---

26   See Mikhail Bakhtin's classic account of this literary history in *Rabelais and His World* [1965], trans. Helene Iswolsky (Bloomington: Indiana University Press, 1984).

Socrates (beyond dispute the prince of philosophers), says amongst other things that he resembled *Sileni*.

Formerly *Sileni* were little boxes such as we can now see in the booths of the apothecaries, decorated all over with frivolous merry figures such as harpies, satyrs, geese with bridles, hares with horns ... and other such paintings arbitrarily devised to make everyone laugh. (Such was Silenus, the Master of good old Bacchus!) But inside were kept rare drugs such as balsam, ambergris, grains of paradise ... and other such costly ingredients.[27]

Rabelais then compares the reader to a dog—citing Plato in calling him "the most philosophical beast in the world"—gnawing on a bone in search of marrow. He then encourages the reader "to be swift in pursuit and bold in the attack, and then, by careful reading and frequent meditation, to crack open the bone and seek out the substantificial [*sustantificque*] marrow."[28] *Substantificial marrow*: a collision of the word *substantial* with *superficial*, or maybe *artificial*, or maybe simply *-ficial*: substance, sub-stance, under-standing, understanding, the surface or face of understanding. Rabelais, a physician who had performed at least one public dissection of a human body in an anatomical theater,[29] knew that

27    François Rabelais, *Gargantua and Pantagruel*, trans. and ed. M.A. Screech (London: Penguin, 2006), p. 205–206.

28    Ibid., p. 207.

29    This dissection was witnessed in 1537 by the Humanist publisher, translator, and eventual Inquisition victim Étienne Dolet (1509–1546). Rabelais scholar Florence Weinberg, author of the extremely interesting study *The Wine and the Will: Rabelais's Bacchic Christianity* (Detroit: Wayne State University Press, 1972), has also written a semi-fictionalized account of Dolet's life which I can only recommend: Florence Byham Weinberg, *Dolet* (Kingsport: Paladin, 2012).

as soon as the bone is cracked, the marrow is no longer "inside," no longer hidden.[30]

This is the light in which to read Hamann's oft-quoted "Reason is language, *logos*—on this bone I shall gnaw myself to death" (ZH 177): not as an announcement of some message or proposition he is trying to convey but as an affirmation that he, too, is still gnawing, still reading, still thinking, searching, generating questions. Hamann is asserting more than the relatively commonplace claim that philosophy is conditioned by its own linguistic constraints: he is attempting to *stage* something in the marrow of language itself, to show that ambiguity is not simply some accidental feature of language but rather something lying so near its heart as to maybe *be* that heart.

To read Hamann is, as Carol Jacobs deftly lays out in her reading of "*Aesthetica in nuce*," to read Hamann as he "reads himself reading."[31] He has no answers for himself, let alone for us: he enacts his own reading and interpretive process on the stage of his texts, a performance very much like what Sylvia Sasse—leaning on two other major theorists of the grotesque, carnivalesque, and "provincial style" (R 5, 5r) of the *khora*, Bakhtin and Kristeva—has called a "theoretical act,"[32] a kind of self-staging theoretical performance art. This process of theoretical enactment does, however, generate clear questions,

---

30    Maybe Kant's definition of humor in *Critique of Judgment*—"an affectation arising from the sudden transformation of a strained expectation into nothing"—gains support *ex negativo* in the fact that I have never found Hamann, or Rabelais for that matter, particularly humorous: their grotesques are too *substantial*, too present in the memory to be nothing. Immanuel Kant, *Critique of the Power of Judgment* [1790], trans. Paul Guyer (Cambridge, UK: Cambridge University Press, 2000), p. 333.

31    Carol Jacobs, *Skirting the Ethical* (Stanford: Stanford University Press, 2008), p. 127.

32    In Mersch, Sasse, and Zanetti, *Aesthetic Theory*, p. 109–124.

or set clear parameters—through the process of generating *doubles* and *opposites*.

## (Anti-)Christ and (Anti-)Socrates

Before turning to the *Letter* itself, I feel compelled to address two truisms of Hamann scholarship whose persistence has always struck me as perplexing and sometimes even unsettling. The first is that the Christian conversion experience described in *Thoughts about the Course of My Life* (written in London in 1758, published posthumously [N II 9–54]) is capable of serving as a privileged interpretive key to the rest of his work, *means* more than the events that seem to have led up to it and surrounded it. In *Thoughts*, he describes, following well-established norms of Christian conversion narratives, his descent into a life of dissolution and decadence in London in 1757–58, his resulting despair, his re-reading of the Bible, and finally an allegedly life-changing identification with eversinful Israel which brings him back to Jesus. Post-conversion Hamann is, we are told (by Hamann), different from the rest of Hamann, with its inscrutable and elusive central persona. The second truism is that he unambiguously *identifies* with his Socrates persona, according Socrates a privileged and protected role in his rhetorical universe. These two supposedly sacred masks—Christ and Socrates—have exercised extraordinary influence on his reception. Upon closer scrutiny they become the most tenuous of all—Christ and Socrates are, as often as not, Hamann's *enemies*. This is because Hamann, as writer, *has* only enemies. Let's take these two masks down from the wall and briefly examine them before moving on.

First, Socrates: Hamann, as will become clearer in the following, was essentially a theorist of *power* and *desire*, not *knowledge* or *thought*. Like Nietzsche a century later, or Hobbes and Spinoza a century earlier, philosophy for Hamann was not just one expression of power-seeking among others but rather *the* quintessential expression of this will-to-power as such. To master a body is one thing; to master a mind which will master its own body is another, as any propagandist knows.

For Hamann, the primal scene of philosophy is not the allegory of the cave in *The Republic*—a turn from the blindness of ignorance to the illumination of knowledge—but Alcibiades' drunken speech in the *Symposium*,[33] cited by Rabelais above (under the title *The Banquet*) as the emblem of satire, which concerns the power of a *master* over the *disciple*—and the Dionysian "madness and frenzy" at the heart of philosophy. In a remarkable scene which throws Socrates' entire project into question, Socrates is confronted by his former pupil and lover Alcibiades, who shows up drunk to the party "crowned with a bushy garland of ivy and violets and with an abundance of ribbons tied round his head,"[34] marking him as acting in the name of Dionysus. The highly sexual nature of his speech, with its usefulness as a source of information about the institution of pederasty, long occluded the more damning accusation of Alcibiades, namely that he—a wealthy, widely-admired Athenian citizen and notorious personality—had become the *slave* of Socrates, both sexually and intellectually, leading to his corruption:

> He spends his whole life pretending ignorance and teasing people. But when he is in a serious mood and opened up I don't know if anyone else has seen the statues he has inside, but I saw

33    Plato, *The Symposium*, ed. M. C. Howatson and Frisbee C. C. Sheffield, (Cambridge, UK and New York: Cambridge University Press, 2008), p. 53–54.
34    Ibid., p. 51.

23

them once, and they seemed to me so divine and golden, so utterly beautiful and wonderful, that in brief I felt I had to do whatever Socrates told me to do.[35]

Plato seems to want us to read Alcibiades' story as desire gone wrong, *eros* out of balance and proportion, not directed to proper ends; but read more literally, it is a story of obsession and the hunger for knowledge, and a master's callous abuse of his disciple. Alcibiades' speech, like Hamann's writing, is meandering and self-contradictory, giving us no unambiguous route out, but this claim does linger in the air. As Socrates himself points out, Alcibiades makes use of the language and norms of "satyric or Silenic drama"[36] to paint Socrates as a satyric character: "Though you were pretending otherwise," Socrates replies to Alcibiades, "the reason for your entire speech was to make Agathon and me quarrel, because you think I ought to love you and only you … But I saw through it, and the plot of this satyr-play, or Silenus-play, of yours is revealed."[37] The inside of the sileni boxes is different in Plato than in Rabelais: the grotesque paintings on the outside hide "small statues of the *gods* inside."[38] Alcibiades' initial gesture is to subvert the metaphor and maintain that Socrates is satyr through and through, his inside no different from his outside—that he, too, is guided simply by *desire*—for sex and power.

Now Christ: however authentic Hamann's London conversion experience might have been personally (who knows?—he talked a lot about Jesus before then, too, and had earlier

35    Ibid., p. 56.
36    See Frisbee C. C. Sheffield, "Alcibiades' Speech: A Satyric Drama," *Greece & Rome* 48/2 (2001): p. 193–209, here p. 195.
37    Plato, *The Symposium,* p. 62.
38    Ibid., p. 54, emphasis mine.

considered a career as a pastor), the far more interesting question to me is what Hamann was up to in London in the first place, and what might have caused him to write this account of his conversion (which, he claimed, was only intended for his father, brother, and their close friends). The fact that his mission may have been a kind of mercantile espionage[39] has long been in the air; what has not been are a few salient dates and names.

Hamann was sent on the mission in mid-1756 by his close friend Johann Christoph Berens, a wealthy Riga merchant and political actor who himself took a simultaneous trip in the opposite direction to Petersburg,[40] then-capital of Russia (he later served as Riga's envoy in Petersburg), in the midst of the Seven Years' War, to a nation which was at war with Prussia. Hamann arrived in London on April 18, 1757 after a long route along the Baltic coast.[41] In *Thoughts*, Hamann writes of delivering a "memorial" (a statement of facts and requests, a diplomatic term) to the Russian envoy to Britain, thus successfully completing his mission.[42] That Russian envoy was Alexander Gallitzin (1723–1807)[43] who served in London from

39　Josef Nadler, *Johann Georg Hamann 1730–1788: Zeuge des Corpus Mysticum* (Salzburg: Otto Müller, 1949), p. 73.

40　Ibid., p. 69.

41　Ibid., p. 72.

42　Ibid., p. 73. Nadler remains characteristically cryptic here, choosing to pose the question rhetorically: "Is this the education of a trade correspondent? No, if anything is unbelievable and completely improbable, it is this. If it was so simple and nothing else was behind it, then Hamann would have had no reason in his letters to Arend Berens, in his 'Thoughts about the Course of My Life,' and over the whole of his lifetime to make such a state secret out of the matter."

43　*Repertorium der diplomatischen Vertreter aller Länder seit dem Westfälischen Frieden* (Zurich: Fretz & Wasmuth, 1950), II, 314, p. 319–320. For more information on Gallitzin, see Karl W. Schweizer and Carol S. Leon-

1755 to 1762—and *not* the Alexander Gallitzin (1718–1783) identified by Oswald Bayer and Bernd Weissenborn in their critical edition of the *London Writings*.[44]

Shortly thereafter, while Hamann was living it up in London high society gaining experience for his conversion story, the Russian army invaded Königsberg on January 2, 1758. This army incidentally had among its commanding officers this *other* Alexander Gallitzin (1718–1783), the ambassador's first cousin and a member of the same Lithuanian-Russian princely family.[45] The degree to which Hamann was aware from the start of his mission is unclear, but what seems to me undeniable is that he was more intimately and decisively involved in the "interregnum in his fatherland" (W 286) (which we will hear more about at the start of the *Letter*) than has previously been admitted. Having served, wittingly or not, as a secret agent for Russian interests, possibly committing actual treason, might shed some light on his long-running near-obsession with the person of Friedrich the Great. Interestingly, this is the very same Gallitzin family to which the Princess Amalia above belonged (through marriage to another Gallitzin ambassador, Dmitri [1728–1803]), in whose home Hamann spent his final weeks

ard, "Britain, Prussia, Russia and the Galitzin Letter: A Reassessment," *The Historical Journal* 26/3 (1983): p. 531–556.

44    Johann Georg Hamann, *Londoner Schriften*, ed. Oswald Bayer and Bernd Weissenborn (Munich: C.H. Beck, 1993), p. 528.

45    John P. Le Donne, "Appointments to the Russian Senate, 1762–1796," *Cahiers du Monde russe et soviétique*, vol. 16 no. 1 (1975): p. 42. Tracking down the Gallitzins has not been made easier by the many variant spellings of their surname (Голицын). I have chosen to use Princess Amalia's spelling, but other alternatives include Galitzin, Galitsyn, Galitsin, Galizyn, Golitzin, Golizyn, and Golitsin. This could be an interesting line of inquiry for someone who can read Russian—I have come to my limits.

and in whose back yard he was unceremoniously buried amid much scandal.[46]

Again: what *was* Hamann?—Alcibiades, accused of profaning the Eleusinian mysteries (by parodying them in a raucous party at his home), left Athens only to return leading an army against his home city, become the tragic traitor: Socrates was sentenced to death for corruption of youth, perhaps specifically for his corruption of Alcibiades.[47] – –

One aim of this book is to push back against a certain view of "relationality" and "dialogue" in Hamann's work—and in the practice of criticism generally. Describing Hamann's antagonistic provocations as a "challenging" and "playful" call to "co-create Hamann's meaning in partnership with the author himself"[48] is a potentially dangerous misreading of a writer whose method—conceived of from the beginning as didactic[49]—is characterized by sustained rage, aggression, and brutal antagonism towards readers, other writers, his "adversary and archfiend" (*Widersacher und Erbfeind*) (W 362) in Berlin, and ultimately maybe towards all texts. What would it mean to take up this call and enter into partnership with a

---

46    See Goethe's uncharacteristically outraged letter to Nicolovius on July 11, 1819, more than three decades after the fact: "consider his relationship with Princess Gallitzin, who dragged him to Münster (which was *not* right!), in whose house (just as wrong!) he died, but so stubbornly the heathen and protestant (!) [*so hartnäckig heidnisch-protestantisch (!)*] that they had to bury him against his will in a corner of the garden (!)" (as cited in Th. C. van Stockum, "Goethe und Hamann: Prolegomena zu einer Monographie," *Neophilologus* 42/1 [1958]: p. 304.) Hamann's body was eventually exhumed and relocated to the Überwasserfriedhof of Münster, where his grave can still be found.

47    See introduction to Plato, *The Symposium*, p. xxvii.

48    Gwen Griffith Dickson, *Johann Georg Hamann's Relational Metacriticism* (Berlin: de Gruyter, 1995), p. 27.

49    Letter to Johann Gotthelf Lindner, September 11, 1759 (ZH 160).

writer who intentionally miscites and disfigures the language of his opponents (after arguing for a real equivalence between text, author, and physical body), who implants impossible-to-solve codes and puzzles into his texts, who is almost pathologically obsessed with alchemy, the occult, and Freemasonry, who makes not-so-subtle allusions to ritual cannibalism in the court of Friedrich the Great[50] (to name one particularly alluring example), associating such a claim with Friedrich's already then well-publicized homosexuality, a writer who, ultimately, in his final work, accuses his enemies in Berlin— most conspicuously Moses Mendelssohn—of belonging, in the words of his primary (and incidentally often misquoted, inverted, and mutilated) source text, the Bible, to "the synagogue of Satan"?[51] What about those weird if intriguing hints that he might quite sincerely conceive of his texts as magical spells or talismans?[52] Maybe a certain affection for neglected, out-of-the way figures, or a certain desire among literary theorists and his disciples in theology for a way to circumvent "Enlightenment" has led his readers to bracket or repress the more unsettling elements of his writing.

Hamann—like Luther before him—is a *diabolical* writer in the fullest sense of the word: his intention is to sow discord

---

50 W 326, note 23, concerning the "precise connection between the culinary arts and religious power" in connection with Friedrich's "setting aside the Eleusinian state secrets" in his poem "Au sieur Noël." The poem was dedicated to his personal chef André Noël, who made a famous dish—called "The Bomb of Ashurbanipal"—so delicious that Friedrich thought it better not to inquire too closely about its ingredients. Johann Wilhelm Gleim's very free translation, the one referenced by Hamann, draws out many of the latent insinuations of certain secret ingredients in the dish (R II 73–76).

51 W 347, quoting Revelation 3:9.

52 What does he mean, exactly, that he hopes that the *Letter* will effect his vacation request (ZH 1024)? Or what about those spirits he conjures in his letter to Jacobi (ZH 1060)?

(the *diabolos* or Accuser being the double of the *symbolon* or Advocate, as in Luke and Revelation[53]), which he does in the register of the *lie* and from a stance of *duplicity*; he is a theorist of the *d(a)emon* (named "Scheblimini" in the Luther-Hamann universe) with powerful consequences in the history of Romanticism (and the politics of Romanticism); and, textually, he is exclusively adversarial, has nothing but enemies—which quality, *Feindschaft,* enmity, Hegel in his lectures on aesthetics proposes as precisely the distinguishing feature of *satire*, that mode or genre which "traditional theories have never been able to make sense of, remaining always at a loss as to how to classify it"—the "artform which assumes the shape of the erupting opposition between finite subjectivity and dissolving appearances" which is the "transitional form" on the threshold between the "Classical" and the "Romantic."[54]

Hamann's attitude towards his critics is the same attitude of Luther towards his in one of his own "flying letters," the *Open Letter on Translation* (1530) where he defended his interpretation and translation of the Bible. I have thought of it often while writing this:

> For we have no intention of being the papists' students or disciples but rather their masters and judges. We'd also like for once to be proud and boast along with these jackasses. And as Paul boasted at the expense of his mad saints, I want to boast at the expense of these asses of mine: They're doctors? So am

---

53    Here I am reading Luke 2:19 and Revelation 12:9 together: the heart of Mary as the site of the σύμβολον (*symbolon*), of bringing together (of human and divine), and the Dragon of Revelation as διάβολος (*diabolos*).

54    Georg Wilhelm Friedrich Hegel, *Ästhetik*, ed. Friedrich Bassenge (Berlin: Aufbau, 1955), p. 491–494.

I! They're erudite? So am I! They're preachers? So am I! They're theologians? So am I! They know how to argue? So do I! They're philosophers? So am I! They're dialecticians? So am I! They're lecturers? So am I! They write books? So do I!

And I want to boast *even further*: I can interpret psalms and prophets – they cannot! I can translate – they cannot! I can read scripture – they cannot! I can pray – they cannot! And to debase myself to their level: I am better at their own rhetoric and philosophies than all of them put together![55]

Hamann, released from the anxieties of his Christian and Socratic apologetes, is a much more disturbing and far more interesting thing, curled, both nourishing and feasting, Behemoth and Leviathan at once (what else would the Serpent be?), around the roots of German literature and philosophy as we have known them.

55   Martin Luther, *Ein sendbrief D.M. Lutthers. Von Dolmetschen und Fürbit der heiligenn* (Nuremberg: Rottmaier, 1530), p. 5. Facsimile of first edition available at: https://www.literaturportal-bayern.de/images/lpbblogs/redaktion/gross/SendbriefDolmetschen.pdf

## 2.  The Dithyrambic Mode:
   A Secret History of Hamann

The *Letter* is loosely organized according to a past–present–future or *memoria–ratio–phantasia* schema, just like the theory of the virtual at its heart: an account of the past is followed by an engagement with the present is concluded by a vision of the future. My reading will follow this schema.

Hamann begins by taking us back—in the third person, through the "Socratic Memorabilia Writer"—to the very beginning. For Hamann, for whom everything is always saturated with everything else, this means taking us back both to the start of his public career as a writer in 1759 and, more ambitiously, to the origins of philosophy, prose, and satire in Athenian theater and Roman verse, via a cryptic set of texts which have intrigued philologists and theorists of language from Horace to the Saussure of the anagram notebooks:[1] Saturnian verse and the *saturae* or satires which emerged in response to it. It is a story of theater's translation to paper, the emergence of reading from watching—which is also a story of the relationship between (Greek) satyr plays and (Roman) satire, between theater and theory, country and city, slave and master. The *Letter* begins:

---

1    The classic introduction to this still-unaccountable project, a study of metrics, coupling, repetition, alliteration, and ultimately anagrams/ hypograms and supposedly secret laws of counting in Saturnian verse specifically and, then, Latin verse generally, is Jean Starobinski's *Les mots sous les mots: Les anagrammes de Ferdinand de Saussure* (Paris: Éditions Gallimard, 1971). In English: *Words upon Words: The Anagrams of Ferdinand de Saussure* (New Haven and London: Yale University Press, 1979).

More than twenty-five years ago, somebody dedicated the first fruits of his authorship to *Nobody the Well-known* in a formal address. The writer was enjoying, at the time, after a journey undertaken out of mutual friendship, and a few temptations abroad, the happiest rest and leisure in his father's house; among whose nearest neighbors was a young bookseller, who brought the manuscript with him to the Leipzig Book Fair and died on the way of a feverish illness. The bookshop, which could not have found an embryo of four sheets in small octavo all that important, received, without giving it another thought, on Christmas Eve of 1759, the first copies of *Socratic Memorabilia*[1] from a printer from Halle, with the message: that the censor at the Academy in Berlin had to be consulted first; through which the press's work was delayed. (W 284, 286)

As at the beginning, so at the end, as *alpha* so *omega*: Hamann is signaling that his authorship—at least—is coming to its end. Like the Saturnians, whose work mainly survives as short cryptic epitaphs on Roman tombs,[2] or like Horace in his testamentary ode "More Lasting than Bronze" (*Odes*.III.30), or Don Quixote on his death bed, or Chaucer on his, Hamann, in this his 24th (or is it 25th? or 26th?)[3] work intended for publication, will compose his own testament, panegyric, epitaph: *non omnis moriar*, not all of me shall die. At a certain point, his testament and epitaph *become* his tomb.

---

2    Hamann in his notebooks demonstrates a notable interest in these Latin epitaphs: e.g. N V 157, 159, and esp. 209.
3    In a letter to Wizenmann on July 22, 1786, Hamann writes something I still have not been able to work out: "So I wanted to play a little fraud, for which purpose a friend offered up his services whose thoughts I would have presented as my own until the matter was developed" (ZH 999). And how do we class his memorial to envoy Gallitzin?

Because the *Letter*'s composition process is unusually well-documented for the era,[4] we can often pinpoint when specific passages were written, sometimes to the day or hour, and observe how they interact and overlap with private letters written during the writing of the *Letter* (primarily to Jacobi), how specific phrasing and content which first shows up in letters ends up in the *Letter* and vice-versa. This presents a rather unique opportunity to observe epistolary intermingling and overflow—of vocabulary, concepts, figures of speech and thought—between two sets and types of texts, private letter and open letter, two fields which become ever more difficult to disentangle.

A specific chronology does emerge which will become forensically important as we observe Hamann altering critical cited texts over the course of composition. This opening passage, for example, was almost certainly written on or around Christmas Eve of 1785. On December 13, he is still testing the waters with Herder: "I am also thinking about my farewell audience with Nobody, the Well-known"; does Herder think "a disrobing and transfiguration of the preacher" might be worth it? (ZH 905). The next day, December 14, Hamann is still just "thinking about concluding my little authorship" "with a flying letter" to "Nobody, the Well-known" (ZH 906). But by December 24 he was fully immersed in a draft of the first five pages (R 2, sent January 1 or 2), as we read in a letter to Jacobi:

---

4    For more on the complex intricacies of manuscript transmission and what constitutes the "text" and its "versions"—a topic I have largely side-stepped—, see Janina Reibold's introduction to the *Historisch-kritische Ausgabe* (R II 8–41), or her English-language summary "Philological Challenges of Hamann's *Fliegender Brief*" in *The Future of Philology: Proceedings of the 11th Annual Columbia University German Graduate Student Conference*, ed. Hannes Bajohr, Benjamin R. Dorvel, Vincent Hessling, and Tabea Weitz (Newcastle: Cambridge Scholars Publishing, 2014), p. 98–119.

Provide me, dear J., with a good suckling nurse for the untimely birth of my Saturnian fatherhood. You should receive the little *phosphorum* from my *s.v. vulua* as warmly as he's coming out of me [*so warm wie er mir abgeht*], but please confirm to me in writing its proper reception and transport into the realm of the black arts of life. The manuscript that I have dedicated to you as a Christmas or New Year's gift is not a children's game but the entire treasure of my head, my heart, and all of my innards, pudenda not excluded. So comply with or answer my impatience soon. (ZH 910)

"More than twenty-five years ago" is thus actually *twenty-six* years ago, possibly to the exact day.[5] A curious account for the theologians' Lutheran saint to write on Christmas Eve: "Phosphorus" is the Greek name for Venus in the morning, the morning star; the Latin translation of the word is, of course, "Lucifer." Grotesque, shocking, and sometimes near-obscene language are Hamann's tools in a way virtually unparalleled in German literature of the 18th century, especially in his bourgeois Lutheran milieu: what we are witnessing is a kind of *Rosemary's Baby*-like birth-to-mastery, and on Christmas Eve at that. (Do we understand yet Kierkegaard's increasingly uneasy sense that Hamann's writing "goes too far, and sometimes has something blasphemous in it, almost as though he

5    Although Jacobi in a note at the bottom of the letter writes "Königsberg 26th Xbr 1785," it is unclear to me whether this refers to a presumed sent date or whether Jacobi believed the dating was a fiction, which is always possible with Hamann. The triplet 24–25–26 is already becoming conspicuous, and could very well be a kind of numerological game the two are playing with each other, or that Hamann is playing with the reader, or himself. Either or all readings seem possible to me.

wanted to tempt God"?[6]—I wonder sometimes whether our sense of Hamann's obscurity is based at least as much on an *unwillingness* as an *inability* to read him.)

What on one plane is a "conclusion" is, on another, stranger, more diabolical plane, an "untimely birth" into his own "Saturnian fatherhood"—the *Letter* as literary double, and a double with a body: capable of being passed (warmly) out of another body, vulva and pudenda and all, capable of fatherhood. No parts of the body are excluded from this bodification of the text; Hamann in fact *insists* upon the inclusion of and emphasis on those parts of the body—breast, vulva, pudenda, innards—which are normally concealed, hidden from light and view, sensible (to the observer) only in states of social exception.

Hamann's letters in the months leading up to this beginning showed an increasing restlessness, a desire for a triggering occasion to write a new and likely final text. He had already found the rough outlines of his subject in the receipt of two books which would come to define the intellectual climate of the coming decade: Jacobi's recently published "Spinoza booklet" (ZH 889) *Über die Lehre des Spinoza in Briefen an den Herrn Moses Mendelssohn* ("On the Teaching of Spinoza in Letters to Herr Moses Mendelssohn") and Mendelssohn's *Morgenstunden* ("Morning Hours"). He was reading both by November 1, 1785.[7] His more general intention, as he tells Jacobi, was "to write something about Spinoza" whose *Ethics* "has been lying on my desk for years and days" (ZH 893 and

---

6    *Papierer* II A 12, as cited in Ronald Gregor Smith, "Hamann and Kierkegaard," *Kierkegaardiana* 5 (1964): p. 63. He also quotes: "Humour can approach the blasphemous. Hamann will rather hear wisdom from Balaam's ass or from a philosopher against his will than from an angel or an apostle" (*Papierer* II A 105).

7    Letter to Johann Georg Scheffner (ZH 887).

891). But it took a specific piece of news to bring things to a boil, to incite his antagonistic mode: a negative book review.

In a letter to Jacobi on November 5, Hamann reports of learning that a review of his most recent work, *Golgotha and Scheblimini!* (1784) is set to appear in the upcoming sixty-third volume of Friedrich Nicolai's influential *Allgemeine deutsche Bibliothek* (*Universal German Library*): "That was water on my mill again – and you can easily imagine how impatient I am to compare my expectations with the enacted judgment; the more annoyed, the more I'll like it" (ZH 889). He anticipates a negative review—"gallows and the wheel for my Golgotha" as he writes to Herder (ZH 891)—from this major organ of the Berlin Enlightenment, which Hamann, borrowing from Mendelssohn's *Morning Hours*, ironically refers to as his "miasmic friend" (ZH 938). He receives his copy on November 27 and, despite his already very low expectations, is nonetheless disappointed: "the entire review is nothing more than a *ridiculus mus* – I had been looking forward to something completely different, and had almost built castles on it ... It seems so tepid to me that I could not even make anything of it – at least no flying machine [*Luftmaschine*[8]] for my journey" (ZH 899).

The review, written by Johann August Eberhardt (1739–1809) but published anonymously and signed simply "F.",[9]

8   Possibly referencing Swedenborg's 1714 sketch of an imaginary "flying machine," although there is a long history of literary fantasies of machines in flight: see Peter Nilson and Steven Hartman, "Winged Man and Flying Ships: Of Medieval Flying Journeys and Eternal Dreams of Flight," *The Georgia Review* 50/2 (1996): p. 267–296. Da Vinci's drawings of his "Great Kite" flying machine were not discovered until the late 19th century.

9   Hamann never learned of the author's identity, though he may have had his suspicions; Eberhardt held Christian Wolff's former professorship in Halle, and was thus indeed a fairly typical representative of established Leibnizian-Wolffian Enlightenment philosophy (R II, 68).

focuses as much on Hamann's style across his whole body of work as on the specific text, reiterating the then already decades-old and still-familiar point of complaint: the use of "cryptic language" full of "far-fetched allusions that often require an erudition and memory that cannot be demanded of everyone."[10] It begins:

> A preacher in the desert, peculiar and strange in clothing and language! But precisely for this reason incomprehensible and cryptic. We can easily distinguish this preacher from his brothers by his clothing and language. We have already gotten used to this about him and have so far tolerated it, despite its lack of appeal for most of us, as it seemed to be more disguise [*Verkleidung*] than clothing [*Kleidung*].[11]

Keep in mind that *Golgotha*, like every one of his other texts, had been published anonymously: his style had *become* his name.

Within the week, Hamann—who was as he reports later "almost overwhelmed by rage" (ZH 910) by the review—had already begun planning his response, latching on in particular to the distinction between *clothing* and *disguise*, *Kleidung* and *Verkleidung*. He writes to Jacobi on December 4: "and so I'm sharing my entire plan with you. I am firmly decided, with God's help, to confound this political review ... My hate for the Berliners and their injustice will not prevent me from imitating their cleverness" (ZH 900). This imitative mode has already kicked into gear by the last paragraph of the same letter: "The preacher in the desert, clothed and disguised, shall disrobe

10    Friedrich Nicolai, ed., *Allgemeine deutsche Bibliothek*, Band 63 (Berlin: Stettin, 1785), p. 20–44, here p. 34.
11    Ibid., p. 33.

himself and attempt to accomplish his transfiguration … as he lies woven between a customs officer [*Zöllner*] and an atheist in the *Univ. Lib.*" (ibid.).

The project is quickly conceived of as a definitive "conclusion" to his "little authorship," at latest by the time he sat down and began writing the December 14 letter to Jacobi: "I stick for the time being to my decision to respond to the Berl. review. There is no shortage of material, but even I myself am unable to master my own reserves. I started with a dedication to Nobody, the Well-known and am thinking of closing my little authorship with a flying letter to him (since that's the main topic in the whole mushy brew) under the motto of the famous saying of Horace: *Non fumum ex fulgure sed– –* " (ZH 906). The Horace is from *Ars poetica* (l.143): "Not smoke after flame but – – " The full passage reads: "Not smoke after flame does he plan to give, but after smoke the light, that then he may set forth striking and wondrous tales—Antiphates, Scylla, Charybdis, and the Cyclops."[12] This is a clue to the kind of theater or theatrics at play in the *Letter*: a burst of smoke *from* which or *after* which emerges light, image, figure: the stagecraft of a magician or actor.

Hamann was only fifty-five years old when he wrote this, was not in particularly ill health, and would not die for another three years—why, then, is he so committed to "closing" his authorship (while keeping the Horace citation open), and at this moment, and what might his apparent failure mean? A question to keep in mind, perhaps, when reading Hamann's plans for the work in this letter, which were not modest:

---

12    Horace, *Satires, Epistles, Ars Poetica*, trans. H. Rushton Fairclough (Cambridge, Mass.: Harvard University Press, 1926), p. 463 (l. 143–145).

God give me the luck and strength to present and bring out [*darzustellen und herauszubringen*] the ideal that's fermenting in my heart: the hair of the reverent reader in Berlin shall stand on end at my gift for clarity, and then they can moan more about the fire than the smoke. ... It's going to be a true *Tractatus Theologico-Politicus* and *Totius Medicinae idea noua* against all previous legal, financial, and exotic [*welsche*] quackeries in the art of governing human beings and states. (ZH 906)

Hamann is rightfully considered an anti-systematic thinker, in the sense that he is not a constructor of discrete, self-operating, internally coherent systems in the mode e.g. of a Schelling or a Hegel. But not all totalizing happens in the framework of systems: as Nancy and Lacoue-Labarthe explored in their early work on the Romantic "literary absolute,"[13] totality and absolutism find a paradoxically amenable home in the fragment. The fragment allows little space for nuance, elaboration, or qualification, and so is well-suited to the totalizing gesture. While not systematic, Hamann is thoroughly *programmatic*: at heart a radical and an anarchist, Hamann aims (at this specific juncture—he will, of course, drift and swerve and reverse, particularly as he comes more and more to antagonize Jacobi, both good-heartedly and otherwise) at nothing more than obliterating the legal, financial, and political system of Prussia as it then existed. (Remember his trip to London?)

It is important to note here that Spinoza appears at the conceptual origins of the *Letter*, specifically Spinoza's political theology in the *Tractatus* (TTP). To this is added a joke, or mask, or hint: *Totius Medicinae idea noua* ("New Idea for a

13    See Philippe Lacoue-Labarthe and Jean-Luc Nancy, *L'absolu littéraire*; *Theorie de la littérature du romantisme allemand* (Paris: Éditions du Seuil, 1978).

Total Medicine") was the title given to a masked re-issue of the TTP (together with Lodewijk Meyer's *Philosophia S. Scripturæ interpres*) in Amsterdam in 1673 under the name of recently deceased physician Frans de le Boë, after the controversial text was banned. A copy of it is noted in Hamann's library holdings in 1776. Spinoza's role in Hamann's late work is hardly researched and yet maybe decisive, as explored in an essay on the *Letter* by Spinozist Manfred Lauermann.[14]

This totalizing program brings us back to the Christmas Eve letter, at the top of which Jacobi later made a note: "Announcement of the Flying Letter." Hamann did not so much recruit Jacobi as a partner in the project as *order* him to carry it out: "A man who has spent 25 years reflecting on himself is allowed to act peremptorily and a bit dictatorially in such an evil and short time" (ZH 910). He demands that Jacobi pay for "nothing more than a rich number of copies for my and your friends *in memoriam*" (ibid.).

More than simply providing funding and logistical support, Jacobi will, as correspondent, shape its outcome: "You know my entire plan, and I have made you a participant in it, an intimate part of it, and expect your support in carrying it out" (ibid.). The *Letter* takes shape in a flurry of letters, manuscripts, and proofs sent between Königsberg and Düsseldorf. The two cities were separated by a postal distance of about twelve days on average, which will become a critical factor later as letters and proofs cross paths. Jacobi was extremely occupied with his dispute with Moses Mendelssohn

---

14    The only study I know of which addresses the direly under-researched Hamann–Spinoza connection in any depth. Manfred Lauermann, "Die Spinoza-Spur bei Johann Georg Hamann," in *Nomaden. Interdisziplinäre 'Wanderungen' im Feld der Formulare und Mythen*, ed. Andreas Leutsch (Bielefeld: transcript, 2003), p. 151–187.

(who would die in early January) and his allies over Lessing's alleged "Spinozism"—an accusation which slightly annoyed Hamann: "You made Lessing a Spinozist without consulting me in the slightest" (ZH 900)—but accepts taking over the financial and logistical burden of publishing the project.

Once Hamann does start writing, it is intense:

> I am now taking my farewell audience from Nobody the Well-known, and the kettle of my burning brain is foaming so terrifically that I need both hands to skim off the dross and keep it from overflowing. You've never read anything as wild [*Panisches*] as this, not in Rabelais, not in Tristram Shandy – It is no longer the voice of a preacher in the desert but rather of the three-headed hell-hound Cerberus. It's a true baptism by fire which will rain down on the philosophers and Chaldeans in Babylon. No *Jupiter pluvis* as in the *Appendix to Socr. Mem.* but a rain of brimstone over Sodom and Gomorrah. I am almost overwhelmed by rage, which is throbbing and raving in every one of my veins, and am frightened by my own power, which is like a violent fever, and seems unnatural even to me. (ZH 910)

Hamann ends the Christmas Eve letter with the following thoughts: "To be or not to be – Non omnis moriar. ... Aut nil aut παν" (ibid., English in the original). Is it "Either *nothing* or *all*" or "Either *nothing* or *Pan*"? A footnote to the second paragraph of the *Letter* tells us.

## 3. *Panick*:
## The Force of Fiction

The footnote occurs in the following sentence which makes up the second paragraph (W 286):

> The Socratic Memorabilia Writer made use of the no less memorable [2] interregnum in his fatherland to oppose his own quackeries [*Saalbadereyen*] to the various quackeries of the prevailing critics and writers who imagine "they know the line they have to hold" — for the benefit of those readers who are still searching and asking, or waiting; because he has now and then been forced, in such a mixed and ambiguous mood, with such a poetic feeling for historical truth, to cry out:
>
> *O! – – ! – – ! vt mihi saepe*
> *BILEM, saepe IOCVM Vestri mouere Tumultus!*
> HOR. I. Epist. XIX.

The footnote runs:

> 2) – – διδασκῦσι γαρ <u>ισα λεγειν</u> 'ὅτωσι ΣΟΦΟΙ.[1] See Plato's Banquet p.m. 320. The wisest critics have unknowingly been spitting at their own pudenda in my *Schediis Lucilianae humilitatis*; since the Panic Style (Sam. Johnson's Idler No. 36) and Magian Manner,
> 
> *– – – qui pectus inaniter angit*
> *Inritat, mulcet, falsis terroribus inplet.* HOR. II.
> Epist. I. 211.

---

1    I have replaced Wilder's transcription with the Greek from Hamann's first manuscript (R 2). Here, as elsewhere, Hamann's Greek (especially diacritics) can be inaccurate, likely because he is citing from memory but perhaps also related to his practice in Hebrew, where the setting of diacritics serves a significant interpretive and religious function. The original passage in the *Symposium* (185c) reads: διδάσκουσι γάρ με ἴσα λέγειν οὗτωσὶ οἱ σοφοί.

was intended, with proper diligence, to be a bogeyman [*Popans*] or caricature of their own dithyrambic mode of thinking and power of judgment. (W 284)

The knot is tied, the talisman charged. A knot with a *dramatis personae*, most still latent, some already familiar, many of whom probably remain to be identified: Socrates, Silenus, Alcibiades, Pausanias, Voltaire, Horace, Lucilius, Petronius, Pan, Samuel Johnson, Anthony Shaftesbury, Richard Hurd, the "wise critics" in Berlin, contemporary philosophers, searching readers, and, finally and most importantly, Dionysus. Scenes and settings: a drinking party in Athens, Horace's country house outside of Rome, Augustan London, Friedrich II's Berlin, the Königsberg of Kant and Hamann, and finally Hamann himself sitting at home at his desk, in his living room.[2]

## Horace

The cited Horace epistle is about imitation and counterimitation, Roman imitation of Greek style, Horace's own imitators, and the role of Bacchus (Liber, Dionysus) in both. Horace had played a pivotal role in reviving the ever-ambivalent figure of Bacchus in Augustan Latin literature, reaffirming the god's role as master of poets and poetic inspiration.[3] In

2    Hamann was a mid-level customs officer and had a small, two-room apartment which he shared with his partner (whom he notoriously never married) and their four children. He was not at all poor, however: the apartment was provided by the Prussian Customs Authority and Hamann had invested most of his money in books and real estate.

3    See e.g. Emily E. Batinski, "Horace's Rehabilitation of Bacchus," *The Classical World* 84/5 (1991): p. 361–378.

this epistle, Horace offers a biting reply to poet-critics who had accused him of being a mere imitator of Greek style by accusing these critics in return of actually imitating *him* to the point of ludicrousness in their overembrace of Bacchus: "no poems can please long, nor live, which are written by water-drinkers. From the moment Liber enlisted brain-sick poets among his Satyrs and Fauns, the sweet Muses, as a rule, have had a scent of wine about them in the morning. ... Ever since I put forth this edict, poets have never ceased to vie in wine-drinking by night, to reek of it by day."[4] The passage Hamann cites with deletions is Horace's most forceful expression of this sentiment: "o imitatores, servum pecus, ut mihi saepe / bilem, saepe iocum vestri movere tumultus!"— "O you imitators, you slavish herd! How often your jesting has stirred my spleen, how often my mirth!"[5] Horace then proceeds to a long boast beginning: "I was the first to plant free footsteps on a virgin soil; I walked not where others trod."

Hamann deletes "you imitators" and "you slavish herd" and replaces them with two dashes each, keeping the two exclamation points while adding one of his own, in addition to capitalizing "spleen" and "jesting." This is characteristic of his citational practice: editing his sources, often through changes in emphasis, thus assimilating them into the dominant voice or persona of the given passage or moment. It also points to one of Hamann's recurring tricks: excluding those words or phrases which would seem most explicitly relevant to the rhetorical moment or citing language preceding or

---

4    Horace, *Satires, Epistles, Ars Poetica*, p. 381.
5    Ibid., p. 383, translation modified. In the following, English translations from the Loeb Classical Library have sometimes been lightly modified into more contemporary English. Here, for example, the translation of "iocum" has been changed from "pother" to "jesting."

following (often immediately) what would seem to be most relevant. This happens at least twice in the second footnote, and reinforces at least four things already observed: a call to closely read and engage with the cited texts, a wink to those in a position to get the joke (i.e. who remember the dashed out words), an ostentatious display of learning, and another added layer of difficulty in accessing the text.

We are already involved in at least five layers of imitation and counter-imitation: Hamann imitating Horace, Horace imitating the Greeks, Latin poet-critics imitating Horace, Horace imitating these poets, mocking them for their imitation with a counterclaim of originality, which imitation Hamann employs to make the opposite counterclaim, that he is *not* original, *not* the source of his style. The layering, mirroring, and flittering accelerates as we read on.

The running text, we notice, is written in the third person while the footnote is in the first person—which remains the case over the first few pages. This use of *grammatical* person to introduce a division within the *authorial* persona immediately brings the question of person(a) onto the stage of the text itself, allowing us to bypass (or more directly address) the question of univocity and intent: the text's voice itself is double from the first. Jacobi's amanuensis Heinrich Schenk (1748–1813), who was given permission by Jacobi to add his own comments on the draft, complains about this, thinking it bad style (R 4, 1r). Hamann replies: "Even if I'm writing my flying letter like a snail or a sloth, I'm nonetheless a brisk *grammaticus* in going from one person to the other. In the notes the 1$^{st}$ and in the text the 3$^{a}$ *persona* speaks, and it's staying that way. I also switch from 3$^{a}$ *persona* to 2$^{dam}$ in the holy maledictory apostrophe to the Well-Known Nobody, whose name, also as *persona poetica*, should rather be *indeclinabilis* than *mobilis*" (R II 167). Double from the first, then triple, and the second person, the third person to appear on the stage is You, i.e. the addressee, i.e. us or someone else. The indeterminacy of pronouns remains a theme throughout the text.

## Pausanias

The semi-cited Plato passage (*Symposium* 185c: "those experts in rhetoric [*sophoi*] teach me to speak in this balanced way") is an ironic comment on the (here dashed out) preceding clause "Pausanias came to a pause"—again indicated only by the double dashes, the underlining and capitalization again being Hamann's emphasis. That clause, a play on words in Greek, reads *Pausaniou pausamenou* and refers to the Sophists' emphasis on assonance and acoustically "balanced" speech.[6] The footnote, itself a pause in the flow of typesetting and sequential reading, is conspicuously placed directly before the word "interregnum."[7] In his editorial comments on the manuscript, Jacobi wonders about the use of this word: "What are we to understand by this interregnum? – It makes the whole passage obscure. The note does nothing less than clarify the issue" (R 4, 1r–1v). Hamann in his response letter writes: "The interregnum was the Russian era of 1759, wasn't it? because my chronology is pretty worm-eaten" (ZH 936)— an interesting response considering the "memorable" nature of that interregnum, and the fact that the previous paragraph was specific enough to mention his receipt of the proofs of his

6    See Plato, *Symposium*, p. 17, note 76.
7    That this placement was intentionally unusual is also suggested by its different placement in the first handwritten draft, where it is in fact placed after the word "less" (R 2, 1v). He moved it forward in the second draft, which was taken up into the proofs and into later editions.

first book on "Christmas Eve of 1759" (W 284). (Remember he was writing this on Christmas Eve of 1785...)

Back, again, to the Russian occupation of Königsberg from January 2, 1758 to May 5, 1762 during the Seven Years' War, a surprisingly liberal period in which intellectual and commercial exchange flourished among the Baltic bourgeoisie (R II 146). It was a state of exception with colossal political consequences, the most relevant for Hamann being the introduction of the so-called *régie* taxation scheme to pay off war debts, which was immensely unpopular across the political spectrum in Prussia, but particularly in Königsberg with its large and prosperous merchant class.[8] Maybe the unusual placement of the footnote points towards this gap: Hamann's decade-long pause in publishing from 1762 to 1772. Apart from his short contributions to the *Königsbergische Gelehrte und Politische Zeitung* from 1767 onwards, this was largely a time of silence and travel for Hamann.

Hamann's response to Jacobi takes a form that we should be used to by now: he is playing the fool and can never be trusted. Hamann's letters cannot be cited to clarify Hamann's authorial persona. First stylistically: Who answers a question asking for simple factual clarification with a question, *wasn't it this?* (He did not change the passage in later revisions.) Then in content: he knows the chronology perfectly well. We see him, in the surrounding paragraphs, over the coming pages, meticulously noting dates and places, cataloguing his entire body of work by date.[9]

8    Florian Schui, "Taxpayer Opposition and Fiscal Reform in Prussia, c. 1776–1787," *The Historical Journal* 54/2 (2011): p. 371–399.
9    Here as ever, it is necessary to keep the reading open for any other other Pausaniases we might encounter in the record, particularly the Greek geographer (c. 110–180 CE) whom Hamann so often cites but also (for example) the Spartan general accused of conspiring with the enemy Persians (d. 477 BC),

## Johnson et al.

Hamann's term "Panic Style" (consciously capitalized; cf. previous draft R 2, 1v, where "panische" and "magische" are both uncapitalized) is his translation of Samuel Johnson's comments in the cited *Idler* paper from December 23, 1758[10] about a specific style of writing he termed the "terrifick," "repulsive," or "bugbear style":

> There is a mode of style for which I know not that the Masters of Oratory have yet found a name, a style by which the most evident truths are so **obscured** that they can no longer be perceived, and the most familiar propositions so **disguised** that they cannot be known. Every other kind of eloquence is **the dress of sense**, but this is the **mask**, by which a true Master of his art will so effectually **conceal** it, that a man will as easily mistake his own positions, if he meets them thus **transformed**, as he may pass in a **masquerade** his nearest acquaintance.
>
> This style may be called the ***terrifick***, for its chief intention is to terrify and amaze; it may be termed the ***repulsive***, for its natural effect is to drive away the reader; or it may be distinguished, in plain English, by the denomination of the ***bugbear style***, for it has more terror than danger, and will appear less formidable, as it is more nearly approached.[11]

especially in light of Alcibiades' likewise joining the Persians to wage war on Athens after successful military campaigns against Sparta.

10    The *Universal Chronicle* began to publish Johnson's *Idler* papers on April 15, 1758, just a few months before Hamann left London on June 27, 1758. (Andrew Sanders, *Short Oxford History of English Literature* [Oxford: Oxford University Press, 2004], p. 331.)

11    Samuel Johnson, *The Idler. By the Author of the Rambler*, vol. I (London: J. Rivington & Sons and T. Carnan, 1767), p. 203–204. Bolding mine, italics Johnson's.

In his *Dictionary of the English Language* (1755), which Hamann owned (N V 51), Johnson defines "bugbear" as a "frightful object; a walking spectre, imagined to be seen; generally now used for a false terrour to frighten babes." Hamann's selected translation, *Popans* (an alternative spelling of *Popanz*), is similarly defined in Adelung's *Wörterbuch*.[12]

Johnson's "false terrour" is an exact counterpart to the *falsis terroribus* in the Horace epistle cited by Hamann. The cited passage is an aside, deviating from the primary theme of lamenting the public's bad taste in poetry and theater; Horace offers praise for those writers whose talent for fiction or illusion is powerful enough to inspire "falsis terroribus" in him:

> ille per extentum funem mihi posse videtur
> ire poeta, meum qui pectus inaniter angit,
> irritat, mulcet, falsis terroribus implet,
> ut magus, et modo me Thebis modo ponit Athensis.[13]

---

12 "[E]in Schreckbild, womit man die Kinder zu fürchten macht, besonders zu manchen feyerlichen Zeiten, daher es auch wohl überhaupt von einem jeden Schreckbilde *ohne Wesen* gebraucht wird [emphasis mine]." The definition also adds an element of etymological speculation: "...wobey man nothwendig an das Lateinische *Peolus*, ein Schleyer, denken muß: so stehet es dahin, ob nicht die *Verkleidung* zu diesem Nahmen Anlaß gegeben" (Johann Christoph Adelung, "Der Popanz," *Versuch eines vollständigen grammatisch-kritischen Wörterbuches der Hochdeutschen Mundart, mit beständiger Vergleichung der übrigen Mundarten, besonders aber der oberdeutschen*, dritter Theil, M – Scr. [Leipzig: Breitkopf, 1798], p. 808–809, emphasis mine). Adelung's dictionary was published contemporaneously to Hamann's career, and Hamann was intimately familiar with it, even hinting at potential wordplay in the dictionary in the *Letter* (R 33, 36, 38).

13 "It seems to me that poet is able to walk a tight rope, who with airy nothings wrings my heart, inflames, soothes, fills it with false terrors like a magician, and sets me down now at Thebes, now at Athens." *Epistles,* p. 415 (l. 210–213), translation modified.

Hamann owned (N V 19) a copy of an anonymously-published English-language commentary on this epistle by English contemporary Bishop Richard Hurd (1720–1808), where it receives the following remarkable gloss:

> 211.—QUI PECTUS INANITER ANGIT,] The word *inaniter* as well as *falsi*, applied in the following line to *terrores*, would express that wondrous force of *dramatic representation*, which compels us to take part in *feigned* adventures and situations, as if they were *real*; and exercises the passions with the same violence, in *remote fancied scenes*, as in the *present distresses of real life*. ... The poet, in the place before us, considers it as a kind of magic virtue, which transports the spectator into all places, and makes him, occasionally, assume all persons. The resemblance holds, also, in this, that its effects are instantaneous and irresistible. Rules, art, decorum, all fall before it.[14]

Conspicuously, Hamann—famously nicknamed "the Magus of the North"—does not include "ut Magus" ("like a magician") in his footnote. But there is another crucial text which does, a major and recurring reference point for Hamann: the second essay of Anthony Shaftesbury's *Characteristicks* (1709),[15] "Sensus Communis, an Essay on the Freedom of

14   Q. Horatii Flacci, *Epistola ad Augustum. With an English Commentary and Notes* (London: W. Thurlbourn, 1751), p. 103–104, emphasis Hurd's. Authorship attested by inclusion in Hurd's collected works: Richard Hurd, *The Works of Richard Hurd, Lord Bishop of Worcester*, vol. 1 (London: T. Cadell and W. Davies, 1811), p. 397.
15   To give a sense of the slippery, unstable ground in a Hamann footnote, and the risks of indefinitely sliding from reference to reference, but lacking sufficient space to follow this line of flight any further, I will point out that the author of the just-cited Horace commentary, Richard Hurd, published a book—which Hamann also owned—purporting to be a dialogue between Shaftesbury and John Locke about the "magic of travel." The dialogue is a

Wit and Humour," a reflection on the nature and worth of "raillery" and ridicule in criticism, also featuring the notion of language and ideas as masks or clothing which can be put on as parody. Hamann translated the first two essays of *Characteristicks* into German around 1755, although he never published them (N IV 474). He mentions Shaftesbury in a long letter to Jacobi on February 15, 1786, where he begins by offering a curious form of encouragement to Jacobi in his planning of a response to Mendelssohn's *To the Friends of Lessing*: "This morning I reread the last will to Lessing's friends. You have at least one mask you can stick with" (ZH 933), linking him with the mask and masquerade theme of his own project: "and everything ultimately boils down to a masquerade in the end" (ibid.). We know from a letter to Scheffner that he was rereading Shaftesbury as late as December 9, 1784: "the English original is presently lying on my table" (N IV 475)—a sign of the significant and enduring influence of Shaftesbury on Hamann, noticeable especially in the concept of "philosophical rhapsody" and the use of "letters" to the public as an essay form.[16]

In a passage in "Sensus Communis" dealing with the nature of fiction, Shaftesbury cites the same Horace passage:

> This Lesson of Philosophy, even a Romance, a Poem, or a Play may teach us; whilst the fabulous Author leads us with such pleasure thro' the Labyrinth of the Affections, and interests us,

---

fictional dialogue, although not marked as such, and was written to parody Shaftesbury's own use of the fictional dialogue as a form of parody.

16    Cf. "The Moralists, a Philosophical Rhapsody" (1709). Exploring the numerous and intriguing traces of Shaftesbury's influence on Hamann goes beyond the bounds of this book, but is a fascinating topic in its own right worthy of more exploration.

whether we will or no, in the Passions of his Heroes and Hero-
ines:

> — — — Angit,
> Inritat, mulcet, falsis terroribus implet,
> Ut magus.                              Hor. Epist. I. lib. 2

Let poets, or the Men of Harmony, deny, if they can, this force of
*Nature*, or withstand this *moral Magick*.[17]

The description of fiction and its "false terrours" as a "force
of *Nature*" and an *irresistable* "moral *Magick*" approaches the
heart of Hamann's understanding of fiction and the virtual
and their role in criticism, and perhaps the heart of fiction and
the virtual as such: the Latin term *virtus* has lived three paral-
lel lives in the history of thought, in physics (virtual, effective,
or violent *force*), in ethics (in the notion of *virtue*, the ethics of
effect or habit), and in epistemology (its role in *perception*, the
main surviving sense, e.g. in digital "virtual reality").

There is, moreover, a persistent but somewhat enigmatic
connection between the virtual and violence, most explicit
in the physical concept of virtual force (in which it is perhaps
rooted), but also in ethics (the disciplining and punishing of
self to generate an effect or *habitus*), and in perception, in
the "shock of recognition," the sudden "terrifick" detection
(or suspicion) of a disparity between being and appearance,
or between countervailing appearances—the face behind
the mask. Hamann, with or via Shaftesbury (at least), shows
the convergence of these three strains of the virtual—natural
force, moral magick, fabulous perception—in *fiction*, through
an encounter with what Virginia Woolf referred to as the "sud-

---

17    Anthony Ashley Cooper, 3rd Earl of Shaftesbury, *Characteristicks of
men, manners, opinions, times* (1711), p. 136, emphasis Shaftesbury's.

den violent shock" and "trance of horror" at fiction's origins, the "revelation of some order" or "some real thing behind appearances"[18] which is not separate from but *completed* by fiction, a real which only *becomes* real through the violent act of fiction,[19] fiction not discrete from but existing elsewhere on a dynamic continuum[20] between the "real thing" revealed by "terrour" and the "false terrours" (counter)acting upon that "real thing" through, for example, "the forces of an opposed elasticity."[21]

The *Letter* is an openly violent text—in conception, composition, and on a textual level. Hamann's prophetic tone is (also) an imitation of the biblical prophets—those "voices crying in the wilderness"—and, ultimately, the god of these prophets himself, the same one speaking in the final lines of Psalm 137 (cited by Hamann 10 times across the project, more than any of the other 13 psalms cited, including Psalm 110, containing the "Scheblimni" of the title of his previous book, which he claims to be defending): "Daughter Babylon, doomed to destruction, happy is the one who repays you

18  Virginia Woolf, "A Sketch of the Past," in *Moments of Being*: *A Collection of Autobiographical Writing*, ed. Jeanne Schulkind (New York: Harcourt, Harvest Books, 1985), p. 64–159, here p. 71–72.
19  For Woolf, writing is an act of asserting power over being: "I make it real by putting it into words. It is only by putting it into words that I make it whole; this wholeness means that it has lost its power to hurt me; it gives me, perhaps because by doing so I take away the pain, a great delight to put the severed parts together" (ibid., p. 72).
20  Cf. Leibniz's argument against discrete space in favor of continual space in "Specimen Dynamicum." Gottfried Wilhelm Leibniz, "Specimen Dynamicum," in *Philosophical Papers and Letters*, ed. Gottfried Wilhelm Leibniz and Leroy E. Loemker (Dordrecht: Springer Netherlands, 1989), p. 435–452.
21  W320, language also borrowed from Leibniz, *Specimen Dynamicum*, p. 447: "*[A]ll rebound arises from elasticity*, and a reason is given for many brilliant experiments which show that *a body is bent before it is propelled*" (emphasis Leibniz's).

according to what you have done to us. / Happy is the one who seizes your infants and dashes them against the rocks" (NIV).

This is fully infolded into the fabric of Hamann's disguises, veils, and masks and the "sledge-hammer force of the blow"[22] of fiction and the virtual, condensed in an almost too-apt manuscript change in an early draft, where "veil" is crossed out and replaced with "power"—right, coincidentally, below the word "darkness":

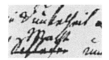

Figure 1: Universitäts- und Landesbibliothek Münster, N. Hamann, 1.37–4 (=R 5, 5r).[23]

The "darkness" or "obscurity" lying conspicuously on the page above the newly-written "power" is part of the same sentence, one of the most reworked and cryptic sentences in the draft:

> If "One is All"; and if a~~ Nothing~~ can at first glance say, ~~the longer the more~~, or rather Everything: then the obscurity of my language is not just cover for sardonic mockery and crocodilian melancholy [*Wehmut*], but also the ~~veil~~ and εξοσια of the motto given to me by a little fortune teller:
>
> (above "a Nothing": humans ... nothing; above "veil": power)
>
> Το ιαν οφον σοφια
>
> All-too-clever is dumb.
>
> O Laertiade, quidquid dicam, aut erit, aut non!
>
> Hor. II. Sat. V. 58 (R 5, 5r).

22   Woolf, "A Sketch of the Past," p. 72.

23   All manuscript and proof images reproduced with the kind permission of ULB Münster.

The *mask/power* connection is made explicit: "not just cover ... but also veil" becomes "not just veil and cover ... but also power."[24] The "One is All" is Lessing's *hen kai pan* (Ἕν καὶ Πᾶν), the summary phrase or slogan (sourced ultimately in Heraclitus) which became a symbol of his alleged Spinozism/ Pantheism.

Veil, *virtus*, power, Πᾶν: we encounter yet another almost vertiginously dense intertextual swerve and switchback, bringing the thread of the knot back through the loop of Hamann's initial choice of the word *Panisch* over, for example, *erschrecklich* or *abscheulich* as were current (and more precise) in contemporary translations of Johnson's terms *terrifick* and *repulsive*.[25] Mask and Πᾶν and power earn another allusion in the text of the *Letter*, when Hamann accuses "the Universal German Librarian" of "a double misunderstanding, with the ridiculous Ethiopian in the philosophical fable about the wager, of mistaking the mask for the face and the face for the mask" (W 306)—another reference to Shaftesbury's *Characteristicks* and a passage which was also (another slide and swerve) the motto of Mendelssohn's *To the Friends of Lessing*, his (posthumously published) response to Jacobi's Spinozism accusations against Lessing.

The passage wonders about the fate of "a native of Ethiopia" dropped in "Paris or Venice at a time of Carnival, when the general face of mankind was disguis'd and almost every Crea-

---

24    This shift also reflects Luther's 1545 gloss of the cited passage concerning religious veils or coverings, curiously referred to as a form of "Macht": "(Macht) Das ist der schleier oder decke / dabey man marcke / das sie unter des Mannes macht sey / Gen. 3" ("[Power] That is the veil or cover / whereby one can tell / that you are under the power of the Man") (R II 130).
25    See e.g. Samuel Johnson, *Der Müssiggänger, eine Sittenschrift, der Vernunft und Tugend gewiedmet. In zween Theilen. Aus dem Englischen übersetzt. Erster Theil* (Leipzig, 1764), p. 161.

ture wore a Mask," a "universal Confusion of Characters and Persons"[26] which recalls Shaftesbury's account of the god Pan and the etymology of *Panick* (translated by Hamann in 1755 as "Sendschreiben von der Begeisterung" [N IV 131–153]):

> We read in History that Pan, when he accompany'd Bacchus in an expedition to the *Indies*, found means to strike a Terror thro' a Host of Enemys, by the help of a small Company, whole Clamors he manag'd to good advantage among the echoing Rocks and Caverns of a woody Vale. The hoarse bellowing of the Caves, join'd to the hideous aspect of such dark and desart Places, rais'd such a Horror in the Enemy, that in this state their Imagination help'd 'em to hear Voices, and doubtless to see Forms too, that were more than Human: whilst the Uncertainty of what they fear'd made their Fear yet greater, and spread it faster by implicit Looks than any Narration cou'd convey it. And this was what in after-times Men call'd a *Panick*.[27]

Pan is one of Hamann's favorite figures,[28] his name appearing e.g. under an image of a grotesque satyr on the frontispiece of *Kreuzzüge des Philologen*, and on the collection of his writings in French, *Essais à la mosaïque*. All the threads of the above converge in Hamann's notion of the *Panische Schreibart*, or "panick style," and in Pan's companion, Bacchus, who brings in the final clause, and maybe most disorienting of all: what would it mean for Hamann's writing to be a "caricature of their own dithyrambic mode of thinking and power of judgment"? What would it mean to satirize satire? Is his "authorship" entirely a charade, a mask, a disguise meant to provoke

---

26  Shaftesbury, *Characteristicks*, p. 82.
27  Ibid., p. 14–15.
28  See also: Achermann, *Worte und Werte*, p. 153–157.

and expose the intrinsic contradictions and ironies of his 18th century contemporaries—his "Host of Enemies"? The answer to this lies in Hamann's understanding of the mask and the virtual, which lies in the latent conjunction here of *Pan* and *Pantheism* or "Spinozism," i.e. in the dissolution of boundaries, both vertical (transcendence—immanence) and horizontal (between texts, genres, languages, words, definitions, persons, bodies: Pan, of course, was a grotesque, priapic god of nature, wilderness, forest, sex, orgy, the dissolution of norms). This is a conjunction made through citation and reference, via Mendelssohn's and Hamann's shared reference text, Shaftesbury's *Characteristicks*—and a conjunction which leads us right into the heart of late 18th century debates surrounding the relation between being and appearance, debates which still in many ways govern the limits of theoretical discourse. Hamann is a singular and singularly underestimated voice in these debates, with more to say to us than Jacobi or Mendelssohn, maybe more by now than Kant or Hegel.

## 4. Typographical Incisions: Flacius Fulbert

Having situated himself in a specific history of literature and philosophy, Hamann now moves to the specific occasion of his writing: the negative review in the *Universal German Library*. He roots his reaction in an expansive, almost cosmic history of the journal, and one presented as intimately interwoven with his own authorship. "Admittedly somewhat earlier, yet still in the same year"—1759—"an exclusive guild of philosophers, who were at the same time aesthetes and wits, also made use of the epidemic-polemic deluge, and instigated a rather one-sided correspondence 'on the latest literature,'[1] out of whose fertile ashes the *Universal German Library* grew, great, high, and fat, like that tree in the midst of the land that a Chaldean Lord of Lords saw in his palace in Babel in a nocturnal dream – its height reached to the sky and spread to the ends of the whole land" (W 290). Among the thousands of spreading literary and critical branches and leaves of this massive public correspondence, Hamann watches a single one fall and land on his desk: "Only the first half of the cited sixty-third volume has room on my narrow desk as a base [*Unterlage*] for my epistolary gleanings [*Nachlese*] for *Nobody*, the *Well-known*. – To ***him***, yes *him*, the highest **idol** and **ideal** of all writing and vanity, I surrender and banish *myself*" (W 292, emphasis Hamann's).

The choice of the word *Unterlage*—which can mean basis or foundation, but also a writing surface or desk pad, as well

---

1    A reference to the literary journal *Briefe, die neueste Litteratur betreffend* ("Letters on Contemporary Literature"), the predecessor project to the *Universal German Library*.

as document or paper, usually in a legal or bureaucratic context, as supporting evidence—gives a sense of Hamann's remarkable sense not just for the ambiguous double light but for word choice and sentence saturation. A single (half-)volume on a narrow desk serves as (a) the document which will become (b) the figural foundation and (c) source of evidence for his *own* document while (d) literally *lying under* his paper as he writes, a physical writing surface affecting the give and bend of his quill, his speed of writing and clarity, how much ink he uses. *Nachlese*, too, "gleanings" or "after-harvest," is full of associations that will echo later in the text, gleanings in the sense of difficult knowledge gathered from various sources, but also in the sense of harvesting (as in *Weinlese*, grape harvest), gathering the grain or grapes which have been left over from the main harvest. Then a third element appears: Hamann surrenders himself to the public, to the reader, to *us*: his text will then become our *Unterlage*.

This is also the moment of the switch from third person to first person in the running text, and it is emphatic: **him**, *him*, he, the Socratic Memorabilia Writer, was, as someone outside of himself, one branch of this massive, flourishing publishing project and was, to that extent, *not* himself. He is now subjecting himself to judgment, making his case before the impersonal watcher, the omniscient audience—the public as god.

After a digression about his personal health and the death of Mendelssohn (who died almost immediately after Hamann began writing)—"not even in this flying letter should the coherence of my thoughts follow the 'thread' of the plan I made" (W 292)—Hamann comes to the crux: the "threefold review" written by the "windy fellow-traveler" who, publishing anonymously, had signed his review with the simple letter "F."—"as an impenetrable monogram of its manufacturer" (W 296).

Hamann roots the *Letter* firmly and even radically in the specific material conditions of the review, its typography (and hence typology), and its physical position in the sixty-third volume of the *Universal German Library*, where the *Golgotha* review is couched between two other reviews by F., all reviewing responses to Moses Mendelssohn's *Jerusalem, or Judaism and Religious Power* (1783). This company both delighted and irritated Hamann: here on the left is the first review, of *Ueber Moses Mendelssohns Jerusalem* ("On Moses Mendelssohn's *Jerusalem*") by Johann Friedrich Zöllner (1753–1804), a preacher at the Nikolaikirche in Berlin most famous for (ironically) posing the question "Was ist Aufklärung?" in the *Berlinischen Monatsschrift* of December 1783, inspiring Kant to write his famous "What is Enlightenment?" essay.[2] Hamann, Kant's neighbor, makes oblique reference to this further on in referring to "Zöllner the Immature" (W 304). *Zöllner* also means "customs officer" in German—and Hamann was a customs officer. It was also the word for the "publicans" or "tax collectors" in Luther's translation of the New Testament. On the right is the third review, of the anonymously-published *Philosophische Bertrachtung über Theologie und Religion überhaupt, und über die jüdische insonderheit* ("Philosophical Examination of Theology and Religion in General, and the Jewish in particular") by Johann Heinrich Schulz (1739–1823), a preacher in rural Mark Brandenburg known for his unconventional religious views (R II 101).

Hamann immediately crafts this constellation into a typological image, referring to himself and his review in a rambling yet startling sentence. The threefold review is Golgotha and Hamann is crucified on it:

2    Immanuel Kant, "Was ist Aufklärung?," *UTOPIE kreativ* 159 (2004): p. 5–10; see note on p. 6.

A preacher in the desert, who must bear the burden, even more than *Nobody the Well-known*, of his disrobing and transfiguration, after fulfillment of the sacrificial vow, (namely if the gods of the earth are no more than the pure transcendent ideals of their sacrificers), is hanging on the Universal German Golgotha [*allgemeine deutsche Schädelstätte*] between a city preacher and a village preacher in the middle like that bronze "type" ["*Typus*"] which represented [*vorstellte*] a serpent but was not one, and became "Nehushtan" under an audacious king. (W 298)

This strange and indicative moment can give us clues to Hamann's unusual approach to typology, both biblical and otherwise. The "bronze serpent" occurs three times in the Bible. First, in the Book of Numbers (21:4–9), we read that, as punishment for their lack of faith while wandering in the desert (they had asked for water and better food), "the Lord sent fiery serpents among the people, and they bit the people; and much of the people died." The "people" then ask Moses to intervene for them and "Moses made a serpent of brass, and put it on a pole, and it came to pass, that if a serpent had bitten any man, when he beheld the serpent of brass, he lived." Moses here, as elsewhere, is able to intervene in God's will, and even contradict it through his own acts and requests. (In his first draft, Hamann included the phrase "which Moses made" [R 2, 2v], but subsequently struck it out.)

Later, in the Gospel of John, in one of the prototypical moments of traditional typological hermeneutics, Jesus says: "As Moses lifted up the serpent in the wilderness, even so must the Son of Man be lifted up; so that whoever believes will in Him have eternal life" (3:14–15). This is followed by perhaps the most summary statement of Christian belief, particularly in Hamann's protestant tradition: "For God so loved the world, that He gave His only begotten Son, that whoever believes in Him shall not perish, but have eternal life" (3:16).

But add "Nehushtan" to the mix and things become more interesting. The reference is to Hezekiah's iconoclastic reforms as recounted in 2 Kings: "He removed the high places, and brake the images, and cut down the groves, and brake in pieces the brazen serpent that Moses had made: for unto those days the children of Israel did burn incense to it: and he called it Nehushtan" (18:4).

Traditional typological hermeneutics depends fundamentally on two tokens which are made to fit, or "two units assumed to exist simultaneously"[3]: the type and antitype, or the figure and its prefiguration (and/or prefigure and figuration), Old Testament—New Testament, Adam—Jesus, Eve—Mary, Bronze Serpent—Jesus, etc. What happens, though, when a third term is introduced, one moreover which is an act of revision or rewriting *within* the reference text? What happens when a text rewrites itself while being read, particularly a text held to have absolute significance? When a third shard threatens the smooth interlocking of type and antitype?

Initially, the *bronze* serpent is an image which, in being beheld, saves one from *fiery* serpents, from that which it represents, but in a different color or mode[4]—from the wrath of God. Then, a later historical revision destroys this image and erases its meaning, ascribing it to mere superstition or idolatry. John must want us to read the merely double type: Jesus is hung on a cross to be beheld as salvation—from that which he represents, the wrath of God. Hamann was too good of a reader for this, and tended not to repress the consequences of

3    Northrop Frye, *The Great Code: The Bible and Literature* (New York: Harcourt Brace Jovanovich, 1983), p. 80.
4    *Nehushtan* in Hebrew combines both "brass" and "snake."

his reading: adding the later revision would mean that Jesus, too, had become an object of superstition, even an idol and thus would need to be broken to pieces and erased. And now we move to the Calvary of the page on which Hamann hangs crucified: the crucifixion of Jesus is repurposed as a type of *Hamann's* having gotten a tepid review from exhausted readers in Berlin.

The use of the word *type* to refer to his text's physical and typographical position signals a persistent blurring of distinctions between the word's various significations, between figure, image, sign, symbol, and print matter. In referring to the review as "threefold" (*dreÿfache*) and even, in a later draft, as a "triune review" (*dreÿfältige Recension*) (R 38, 1r)—one review, three coequal iterations or layers—he also announces a refusal to read the three texts separately and discretely, to acknowledge divisions between them. He will, in typical fashion, cite from them promiscuously, move fluidly across their textual borders, and integrate their language and vocabulary into his own text, both with and without attribution.

This passage, and Hamann's use of the word *type*, perplexed Jacobi enough to comment on it in his notes on a draft: "The actual meaning of this allegory refuses to reveal itself to me" (R II 4, 1v). Hamann replies: "*Type* has to stay and prepares the passage from *Clouds* you cited yourself, and also has its suggestive sense. No excessive quotation marks. The threefold review will serve completely as basis [*wird überhaupt zu Grunde gelegt*], and I do not spoil lazy readers" (ZH 936).

In Hamann's second book *Clouds: An Epilogue to Socratic Memorabilia* (1761)—the text "cited" by Jacobi—the bronze serpent also appears: " – – yes, the disciple whose boldness emulated that king in Judah who crushed the bronze serpent, which Moses raised up under the strictest orders, and which was a parable of the Son of Man, whom GOD anointed with the oil of gladness above his fellows!" (N II 108) What Jacobi cites is an "anointed idol" (R II 4, 1v)[5] in the next paragraph, where Hamann's attention turns to "the village preacher" whose book is the subject of the third of the reviews. This preacher is Schulz, "a protestant pastor of a flock which is presumably made up of Gadarenes, Menippuses, and Meleagers" which a footnote helpfully informs us are "cynical philosophers according to Dio[genes] Laer[tius], Book VI, §99" (W 300).

Hamann lets us know what he thinks the proper task of the reviewer is:

> The reading of a reviewer is hardly a matter of judgment but instead simply skillfulness in correctly reciting what he has read. Every person is, by virtue of the autonomy of pure reason, or at least its good will, his own nearest lawgiver, and natural judge; every writer consequently judges himself. (W 302)

And makes it clear that his reviewer has failed, and aggressively—and the malicious failure of the reviewer is the initiating point of his disrobing and transfiguration:

> Now arises [*Nunmehr hebt sich...an*] the disrobing and transfiguration of my five sheets with their title, which were however so mutilated and re-healed by a *Flacius Fulbert* on the Universal Golgotha of German Skulls, that no trace remained of my entire miniature authorship and its *Corpusculum delicti.* (W 316)

5     In German "Oelgötze," a polemic term which emerged in the Reformation to refer to Catholic statues and images, but which eventually entered colloquial language as an insulting term for a stiff, silent person (Grimm), a meaning it maintains to this day.

What so bothers Hamann? The failure to correctly recite, and in particular to cite the title and mottos—the *Aufschrift*—of the work, which he sees as a "castration" of the "true *testiculi* of my authorship." By failing to mention or consider the significance of the title, the reviewer has "eradicated and annihilated" "the entire title of my authorship" (R 11, 2r).

Here Hamann introduces one of the primary preoccupations of the *Letter*: the "typical meaning" (R 9, 2r)[6] of titles, mottos, frontmatter, etc. in general as well as an engagement with and critical negotiation of three specific titles (or, in a later draft, "the three-headed title" [R 40, 1v]): *Golgotha and Scheblimini!*, *Jerusalem*, and finally the *Letter*. The ambiguity of *which* title Hamann is referring to at any specific moment is key to detecting certain subterranean shifts[7] that occur within the text and over the course of its composition. It is a preoccupation with astonishing results, as we will see in the next chapter.

This violation of the *Aufschrift* gains figural articulation in a letter to Jacobi in April 1786, through a name and figure who migrates from the letters into the manuscript: Flacius Fulbert. Hamann expresses his intent "with the disrobing and transfiguration of the title to transfigure the Berliner reviewer into a Flacius Fulbert, as he had the audacity to assault the double motto from Deut[oronomy] and Jeremiah with his

6    A phrase imported from the review (p. 35) but not unrooted in Hamann's own typological hermeneutics.

7    Like Pan, god of caves and labyrinths, truth for Hamann is subterranean, a fundamental stance of his as expressed to Jacobi on April 23, 1787 after abandoning the project: "Truth must be dug out of the earth, and not created out of thin air ... but instead first be brought to light out of earthly and subterranean objects [*aus irrdischen und unterirrdischen Gegenständen*—note the unconventional double Rs]" (ZH 1058).

*cultello flaciano*, for these two testimonies [are] the true *testiculi* of my authorship" (ZH 962).

The name *Flacius Fulbert* is a merger of two separate names and images: Matthias Flacius (1520–1575) was a radical Lutheran theologian and famed scholar and book collector who became legendary for disguising himself as a monk to gain access to monastery libraries where he would promiscuously cut out useful manuscript pages with his "Flacian knife" (*cultellus flacianus*) which he then smuggled out of the monastery in his sleeves.[8] He was also one of the most radical proponents of the protestant doctrine of total depravity, holding that "sin is man's substance," a controversy which roiled the Lutheran church and was only resolved in 1577.[9] Fulbert was the uncle and ward of Héloïse who had Peter Abelard castrated in the immensely popular medieval story of the two foiled lovers, preserved in their letters to each other. Peter Abelard was also the author of a banned theological work *Sic et non* ("Yes and No"), a catalogue of apparent contradictions in the church fathers and scripture. Flacius and Fulbert both belong simultaneously to a literary history as well as a history of radicalism, censorship, and dissent.

This nickname, and the startling images it evokes—merging the cutting of paper with the cutting of sexual organs—is

8    See e.g. the entry in the *Allgemeines Gelehrten-Lexicon*: "Er ist vor diesen Verwirrungen in Mönchs Habit unbekannter Weise in den Klöstern herum gegangen, und hat die Historicos heimlich in seinen weiten Ermeln heraus practicieret [...]; daher das Sprichwort gekommen: Cultellus Flacianus, weil er damit immer die kleinen Tractatgen, so ihm angestanden, herausgeschnitten, und in seinen Kleidern versteckt." Christian Gottlieb Jöcher, ed., *Allgemeines Gelehrten-Lexicon*, vol. 2 (Leipzig: Gleditsch, 1750), p. 628–629.
9    "Flacius Illyricus, Matthias," *Oxford Encyclopedia of the Reformation* (Oxford: Oxford University Press, 1996), digitally accessible at oxfordreference.com.

initially a tool of accusation, a naming act or limning of the "factory stamp" F. (The initial Fs in Flacius Fulbert are underlined in the handwritten manuscripts.) The connection between texts and organs, and especially sexual organs, remains thematic.

"A writer," Hamann's argument goes after introducing Flacius Fulbert into the *Letter*, "gives the robes of his nakedness and need such a precision that no clipping, let alone cutting, can appropriately take root without violence.[10] The title of his work is the signature of his name" (R 12, 1r). The garment of the title, text, or type is *cut* in advance (*pre-scission*); incisions or excisions are violent interventions, comparable to the mutilation of a body.[11] Cutting title, text, or type is an intervention in the genetic code (he even adds the word *genetic* in his rewrite: "genetic type" [R 36, 4r]) of the type or text, and thus into the writer's genetic code—her name and signature, even her body. Hamann then uses the metaphors "egg" and "seed" to illustrate the "development" from type, before introducing a less familiar movement of figure, conceiving of the generation and subsequent *de*-generation of title and type in terms of *elasticity*, a concept from solid mechanics first elaborated by Leibniz, drawing parallels to botanical and sexual processes. The passage in full reads:

10   "Ein Schriftsteller giebt dem Gewande seiner Blöße und Nothdurft eine solche Präcision, dass keine *Be*schneidung, geschweige *Ver*schneidung, ohne Gewaltsamkeit füglich angeht." The botanical reading of "füglich angeht" is supported by the following paragraph.

11   In the 1780s, both *Beschneidung* and *Verschneidung* dually connoted both cutting generally and a specific cutting of the body, namely of the (male) genitals. *Beschneidung* circumcision, and *Verschneidung* castration, or in the words of Adelung's *Wörterbuch*: "5. Ein Thier männlichen Geschlechtes seiner Mannheit berauben, entmannen" ("Verschneiden," vol. 4, p. 1127–1128).

The title of his work is simultaneously the signature of his name, and both characters an impression of the signet ring on the divine finger of beautiful nature; which all unfolds from a round egg and the *minimo* of a mustard seed to life-size [*Lebensgrösse*], all in turn rejuvenates, returns, and is accomplished in the very same type, through the forces of opposed elasticity. Such a title is a typical seed, an orphic egg in which the muse has spread out tent and hut for her genius, which emerges from its womb like a groom from his chambers and rejoices like a hero to walk the path to the aim of his winged sense, which already stands sketched [*gezeichnet*] on the forehead and navel of the book. Here, then, is the beginning of his voice and language, whose cord runs on to the end of the speech, that all may be suffused by a single light and fire. (W 320)

This both reflects (in its biotic, procreative referents) and undercuts (in its own figural mechanics) the organicist[12] vocabulary that would soon come to theoretical prominence in Romantic and Idealist poetics around 1800 (a discourse in no small part influenced by Hamann himself), presenting us with a gesture not easily subsumed to the classic mechanic–organic dichotomy. The metaphor of an egg or seed developing into full blossom or *Lebensgröße*[13]—a familiar enough trope—is undercut by the peculiar next step: the *return to type* through "forces of opposed elasticity." The title or type is "a double-edged instrument that liquidates and legitimizes itself, – a Sphinx biferons" (ibid.).

12   See Stefanie Heine, "*Fort-Pflanzung*: The Literary Absolute's Botanical Afterlife," in *Understanding Jean-Luc Nancy, Understanding Modernism*, ed. Cosmin Toma (London: Bloomsbury, forthcoming 2021).

13   Also a reference to his own *Schriftsteller und Kunstrichter; geschildert in Lebensgröße von einem Leser, der keine Lust hat Kunstrichter und Schriftsteller zu werden* ("Writers and Critics; Portrayed in Lifesize by a Reader who Doesn't Feel Like Becoming a Writer or Critic") (1762).

Hamann presents his own texts as *elastic, polyhedral*[14] *solids* and refers to his own style as *plastic*. In an early draft paragraph of polemical self-defense (later heavily redacted), he contrasts "fluid" and "solid" styles with his own "plastic" style: "the fluidity of style, in line with the properties of all fluid bodies" corresponds to "a too light, loose, inconcise coherence of thought, a weakness of their gravity" (R 5, 5r). This is contrasted with an "extremely opposite style" of "a brittle solidity, an overstuffed fullness and hardness" (ibid.).

Hamann's "provincial style" on the other hand—and this account also needs to be read "cum grano salis" (R 16, 3r); it is masked in Kantian language (e.g. "transcendent," "pure," "categories")—functions according to the rules of "exotic plasticity," mixing "clay with the iron's plant [*Thon mit des Eisens Pflanze*]" (R 5, 5r):

> and so maybe it was exactly this kind of impure composition that was the most powerful *organon* for the transcendent material of my indefinite subject, a *caeruleus proteus* susceptible not just to the most variable colors but also to the most contradictory forms, like lightning. The brew [*Most*] of my metacriticism needed newer and purer predicaments and categories than the coinages and windskins of smoke-filled school-foxery [*die Kunstworte und Windschläuche verräucherter Schulfuchserey*]. (Ibid.)

Hamann writes in his letters of his own "optical illusions" (ZH 933) when rereading his text, of chasing "wills o' the wisp"[15] (*Irrlichter*) (ZH 938). The reference text here is Leib-

---

14   From Hemsterhuis's *Lettre sur la Sculpture*, p. 30, added by hand to a late proof (R II 86).
15   Credit for this delightful internal pluralization is due entirely to the ever-attentive eye of Andrew Hamilton.

niz's explication in "Specimen Dynamicum"[16] of elasticity and the collision of bodies (and "opposed elasticity"—though note that return to form is the *removal* of force, its absenting)—developed, curiously, in the context of his remarks about "conatus" (or "virtual motion"; also a central concept in the metaphysics and ethics of Spinoza)[17] and effective or "virtual" force (which he refers to, using Aristotelian vocabulary, as "violent" force), as well as François Hemsterhuis's somewhat cryptic remark in his *Lettre sur la Sculpture* (1769) on "ouvrages à la mosaïque" or "développements de polyëdres" "dont tous les contours sont équivoques."[18]

16    In this text—of immense importance in the history of science—Leibniz, at the request of "many prominent men in various places" explains his "new science of dynamics, which was still to be founded" (Leibniz, *Specimen Dynamicum*, p. 435). Hamann was intensely familiar with Leibniz's work, including in physics. His name comes up in the text itself, and numerous times in the letters. We as readers must, however, remain wary: Hamann lists a few of his planned masks in a letter to Jacobi, including his Leibniz mask: "I will also tell a story with Xenophonic simplicity after I have first prepared the reader a bit with Leibnizian sublimity[,] philosophical ideas[,] and Rousseauvian warmth of eloquence to untangle the knot" (ZH 913). Or actually doubly wary: Hamann here has again borrowed his language from the review (p. 37–38), where Leibnizian sublimity and Rousseauvian warmth are attributed to Schulz by the reviewer.

17    *Conatus*—Latin for "striving, effort, tendency"—was a somewhat enigmatic concept in the history of physics (with similarities to the concept of "inertia," by which it has been completely replaced in post-Newtonian physics) linking three of Hamann's major reference points in this text, all major theorists of conatus: Hobbes, Spinoza, and Leibniz. It was an attempted explanation of the existence of motion, and referred, in Spinoza's definition, to an inner tendency towards self-preservation; Leibniz defined it to deal with the problem of continual space (as opposed to discrete, i.e. Cartesian space) and Zeno's Paradox.

18    "Il y a des objets dont tous les contours sont équivoques, & qui néanmoins plaisent infiniment. Ce sont les bons ouvrages à la mosaïque, & qui sont pour la plus-part des développements de polyëdres. On peut les comparer à un concert de musique, & ce ne sont pas tant des compositions

With this in mind—the intense significance ascribed to title and type, their real equivalence with (solid) body—the revision of the *type* paragraph in the next draft sent to Jacobi (January 18, R 3) becomes extremely conspicuous: the first appearance of "disrobing and transfiguration" as a full phrase in the *Letter* is conjoined to the type analogy above.

Hamann, in drawing our attention to the role and nature of titles, is also of course drawing our attention to the presence of his own title. This is emphasized in the first sentence of the next paragraph, where he turns his attention to Zöllner's book: "I only know Herr Zöllner's text from outside, and by the charm [*Brelocke*][19] of its title" (W 298).

What, then, of Hamann's own title? His remarkable response, as we will see in the next chapter, is to *himself* assume the disguise of Flacius, not only masking himself in his opponent's language, but picking up the Flacian knife and smuggling himself into the reviewer's text where he *finds* his title and then, via a series of manipulations to a single cited passage, transfigures it through the disguised, barely detectable *insertion of his own title back into the (mis-)citation*—an act of citational trans- or disfiguration and source contamination which can on the basis of the existing manuscripts be genetically traced in detail. Hamann, in the course of writing, then implants his own remarkable act of disfiguration *into* the *Letter* as a kind of code or game, as simultaneous "key" and "door and lock" (R 29)—adding a new dimension to his

de parties, que des compositions de touts. Dans cette espèce d'ouvrages chaque partie peut être partie principale, & tient à plusieurs touts différents, réguliers, & parfaits, & le mouvement le plus imperceptible de l'oeuil fait changer l'idée du tout; ce qui produit une richesse étonnante d'objets" (Hemsterhuis, *Lettre sur la Sculpture*, p. 30, as cited in R II 86).

19   From the French *breloque*, a charm hanging from a bracelet, necklace, or watchchain.

repeated references to the "conclusion," "sealing," or "locking up" (*Abschluss*) of his "author role." This disfiguration has profound implications for the significance of the entire project, and of Hamann's understanding of the nature and (non-) limits of texts, citation, and intertextuality in general.

## 5. Disguise and Disfiguration: Hamann Cites a Title

In the first handwritten draft, Hamann begins by making "space enough from both sides" (R 3, 2v) for his response by addressing in turn each bordering review, first Zöllner's and then Schulz's. Concluding a paragraph explicitly concerning the Schulz review ("with his enthusiasm for atheism") Hamann, in a first peculiar gesture, inserts a quote from the *Zöllner* review:

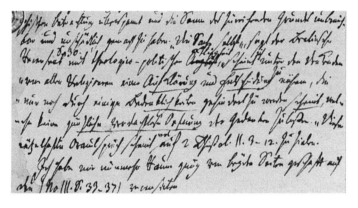

Figure 2: Universitäts- und Landesbibliothek Münster, N. Hamann, 1,30–6 (= R 3, 2v).

„Die Sache selbst,‚‚ sagt der Berlinsche Recensent mit theologischer-politischer ~~Arglist~~ Klugheit, „scheint sich unter den Denkenden von allen Religionen einer Aufklärung und Entscheidung zu nähern, die nur noch durch einige Bedenklichkeiten gehindert zu werden scheint, welche keine gänzliche verdachtlose Oefnung der Gedanken zulaßen.‚‚ Dieser räthselhaften Oraculspruch scheint wol auf 2 Theßal. II. 3–12 zu zielen.

"The matter itself," says the Berliner reviewer with theological-political ~~guile~~ cleverness, "<u>seems</u> among thinkers of all religions to be nearing a <u>clarification</u> and <u>decision</u>, which now <u>seems</u> to be hindered only by several <u>reservations</u> which do not permit of a full, insuspicious opening of one's thoughts." This cryptic oracular utterance seems to be aimed at 2 Thessal. II. 3–12.

The unconventional (mis)placement of this citation prompted Jacobi to complain in his comments on the manuscript: "Because these words are in the review of <u>Zöllner's</u> book, your citation of them here could be interpreted as a <u>misplacement</u>" (R 4, 2r). For reference, the relevant passage in the bordering review—again, not at all addressing Hamann's or Schulz's book—appeared as follows:

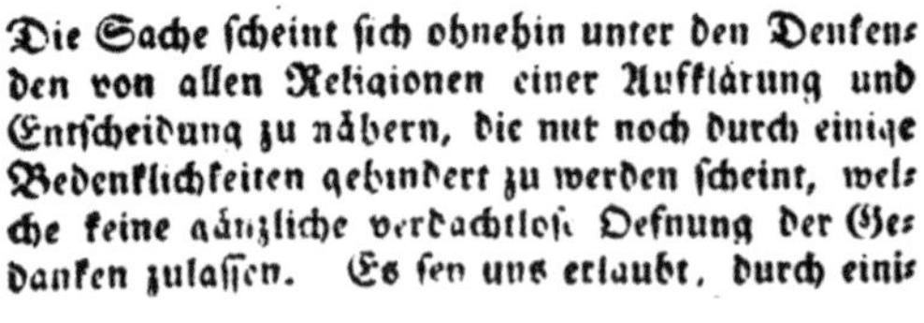

> Die Sache scheint sich ohnehin unter den Denken-
> den von allen Religionen einer Aufklärung und
> Entscheidung zu nähern, die nur noch durch einige
> Bedenklichkeiten gehindert zu werden scheint, wel-
> che keine gänzliche verdachtlose Oefnung der Ge-
> danken zulassen.   Es sey uns erlaubt, durch eini-

Figure 3: *Allgemeine deutsche Bibliothek*, Band 63, p. 30.

Fully aware of and possibly in direct reaction to Jacobi's scrupulous concern with correct citation practices and his familiarity with the source texts,[1] Hamann now does something incredible with the misplaced citation: he replaces the word "Entscheidung" (decision) with "Ent**k**leidung" (disrobing) and then, after initially leaving "Aufklärung" (clarification/ Enlightenment) in place, strikes through *Auf-* and replaces it with *Ver-*, transfiguring the word into *Verklärung* ("transfigu-

---

1    E.g. "Hier müßte nothwendig die abgezielte Stelle in der Allg. d. Bibl. citiert werden," etc. (R 4).

ration"), while dropping "verdachtlose" (insuspicious) from before "Oef[f]nung" (opening) and elaborating the sentence about its "cryptic" character.[2] He furnishes it with more intertextual (biblical) references and inserts the critical word "prophesied," central to his theory of "observation" and "prophecy"—functional equivalents of, respectively, "disrobing" and "transfiguration"—later in the writing process:

Figure 4: Universitäts- und Landesbibliothek Münster, N. Hamann, 1,42–7 (= R 5, 4r).

[*Continued from previous page*, R 5, 4v: Aber auch diese Sache] nebst so mancher anderen „scheint,,, nach einer andertweitigen theologico-politischen Anmerkung S. 30 „sich unter den

2    Reiner Wild did indeed notice this change, but unfortunately failed to ask whether the insertion of the words of the title into a citation in a text *about* titles and citation (and the close reading of both) might be worth further examination, offering instead a quick, two-sentence exegesis: "[Hamann] spricht also diesen 'Denkenden' ab, im Namen irgendeiner Religion zu sprechen. Mit diesen Änderungen und mit den folgenden Hinweis auf Bibelstellen stellt Hamann den festgestellten Atheismus der Aufklärung in heilsgeschichtlichen Zusammenhang, er ist im Zeichen der Endzeit"(W 118–119). The change is mentioned again later, where it is again framed in terms of "Demut vor Gott" (181). Although these are interesting readings, Wild missed his opportunity to understand a crucial later passage concerning nothing less than the "typische Bedeutung meiner Autorschaft" and/or the "typische Bedeutung meines metakritischen Parallelismi," writing: "Der Schluß dieses Abschnitts bleibt dunkel; auch die in Anmerkung 18 genannten Textstellen bringen wenig Licht" (205).

Denkenden aller Religionen auch zu einer ~~Auf~~Verklärung und
Entkleidung zu nähern, die nur noch durch einige Bedenklichkeiten gehindert zu werden <u>scheint</u>, welche keine gänzliche
Oeffnung der Gedanken zulaßen,,. Wovon auch schon St. Paulus
2 Theß. II.3–12 geweißagt zu haben scheint, nach der Weisheit,
die ihm gegeben war, schwer zu verstehende Dinge zu schreiben
2 Petr. III. 15, 16

But this matter, too, alongside so many others, "seems" according to another theological-political remark p. 30 "among thinkers of all religions to be also nearing a transfiguration and disrobing, which <u>seems</u> to be hindered only by several reservations
which do not permit of a full opening of one's thoughts." Of
which St. Paul 2 Thess. II.3–12 seems also to have already prophesied according to the wisdom given him to write things hard to
be understood 2 Peter III. 15, 16

By the fourth (unsent) handwritten formulation of this passage, "Aufklärung" has been completely replaced by "Verklärung" and "Entscheidung" by "Entkleidung." Moreover,
the gesture is *emphasized* by the double underlining of *Ver-*
and *-kl-*, further accentuated by a different and more insistent
curvature than Hamann's normal underlining:

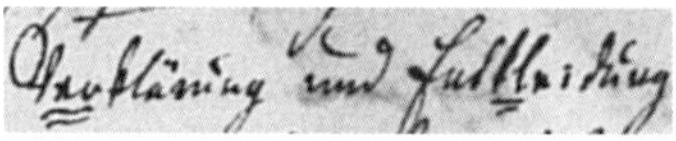

Figure 5: Universitäts- und Landesbibliothek Münster, N. Hamann,
1,44–1 (= R 9, 1r).

The underlining is taken up by the typesetter in the proofs as
letter spacing, a customary form of typographical emphasis at
the time, a subtle difference:

## Verklärung und Entkleidung

Figure 6: Universitäts- und Landesbibliothek Münster, N. Hamann, Bd. 19, 11 (= R 27, 11).

Hamann's gloss of the (mis-)citation also gains a crucial addition. To "things hard to be understood" he appends: "which *confuse* the unlearned and unstable, as well as *the other scriptures*, unto their own destruction" ("welche *verwirren* die Ungelehrigen und Leichtfertigen, wie auch *die andern Schriften*, zu ihrem eigenen Verdammniß") (R 9, 1r, emphasis mine).

Here Hamann plays with a certain ambiguity in Luther's translation of the source text: do these hard-to-be-understood things confuse persons *and* other scriptures/writings? He makes two crucial changes, one lexical and one syntactic, to Luther's translation of the referenced biblical passage (quoted without quotation marks). In Peter's letter the agent of distortion, twisting, or inversion (*Verdrehung*) is plain: the "unlearned and unstable" (KJV) distort the hard-to-understand "things" in the letters of Paul—as well as in unspecified "other scriptures." Syntactically, Hamann's shift of the verb from the end of the clause to a position immediately following "welche" ("which") introduces a destabilizing semantic ambiguity into the sentence—now it is unclear if these "difficult" writings are the *victim* of distortion/confusion (obscuring or distorting a presumed hidden clear meaning) or in fact an *agent* of distortion/confusion. Both possible readings converge, however, in a single factor: in either case, *texts function as subjects* in terms both of grammar and agency, i.e. as entities capable of acting. In Peter's letter, "the unlearned and unstable" are the agents who perform the twisting or distortion of the texts; in Hamann's own *Verdrehung* of the source text, the texts *themselves* become subjects with agency. Hamann is asserting for himself, and/or for his texts, a truly radical right—not merely

79

the use of "hard-to-be-understood" language to confuse *persons* but the right of his texts to actively intervene in and confuse or entangle other texts—including the Bible.

On April 5, Hamann received his first printed proof of the first nine manuscript pages. Throughout the writing process, Hamann insisted upon receiving either proofs or handwritten transcriptions of proofs to continue working[3]—he complains that he cannot read his own writing, and did not make copies of his own texts before sending them off. He emphasizes—almost obsessively later in the writing process, shortly before abandoning it—that he needs the presence of a printed text to organize and refocus his thoughts. The receipt of this first proof marks a substantial shift in the project. At some point between its receipt and April 23, Hamann writes this disfiguration of the source into the main text, as a sort of collaborative—and virtually impossible—game or experience with the reader. First he criticizes the reviewer for committing a kind of April fool's joke:

> Einiger in einem Fuder Heu zerstreuten Stecknadeln willen werden die allgemeinen deutschen Leser April geschickt, oder um 'deutlicher zu reden['], auf alles das 'Wenige' verwiesen,[4] was

---

3    See e.g. ZH 936, ZH 991. In the former he also adds: "I would wish for a good, clear, spacious layout, as my thoughts are pressed so tightly together that they're almost suffocating each other."

4    He is referring to Eberhardt's comments on p. 35 of the *Allgemeine deutsche Bibliothek*, Bd. 63: "Was wir indeß mit Mühe, und nicht ohne Besorgnis zu irren, herausgebracht zu haben glauben, ist *das Wenige*, daß der V. nicht das Eigenthumsrecht in das Recht in Collisionsfällen zwischen Selbstgebrauch und Wohlwollen zu entscheiden will gesetzt wissen, und dass die Absicht der mosaischen Religionshandlungen ihre typische Bedeutung sey" (emphasis mine). Hamann's repeated point—a criticism of Eberhardt as a reader—is that Hamann had composed his book in the language of his subject, using terms like "property right" and "collision

überlängst [in the *AdB*] geweißagt stehn soll ohne daß man weiß, wie diese entlegene, verlorne Anspielungen u Winke zur gegenwärtigen Sache und Person eines Predigers in der Wüste gehören. (R 9, 2r)

For the sake of a few needles strewn in a stack of hay, Universal German Readers are made victims of an April fool's prank, or "to speak more clearly," referred to all of that "little" that is supposed to have long been prophesied [in the pages of the *Universal German Library*] without giving any clue as to how these remote, lost allusions and hints have anything to do with the present matter and person of a preacher in the desert. (R 9, 2r)

He is reiterating his complaint that the reviewer is himself guilty of obscurity and sending the reader on an easter egg hunt for references which were only ever an interim and disposable disguise. He then announces his reaction:

Ich sehe mich daher *gleichfalls genöthigt* meinem geneigten Mitleser, der willigen Herzens ist, ein leichteres und sanfteres Joch aufzulegen, und ihm die weder gefahrliche [sic] noch vergebliche Mühe zuzumuthen, daß er nemlich die seit Monathen auf meinem Pulte ruhende dreÿfältige Recension ... eigenhändig aufschlage, und zu Rath ziehe, um die typische Bedeutung meines metakritischen Parallelismi auf ein Haar zu treffen. (Ibid., emphasis mine)

I therefore see myself equally compelled to lay upon my gentle fellow reader of willing heart a light and easy yoke, and burden

cases" as parody, which is mistaken by the reviewer—and "lazy readers" generally—for his own language and arguments, while the original intention was to *dispose* of the vocabulary by *exposing* its inner contradictions.

him with the neither dangerous nor futile effort of opening up with his own hand and consulting the threefold review that has been lying on my desk for months to arrive precisely at the typical meaning of my metacritical *parallelismi.*

Hamann here places an almost—if not entirely—intolerable demand on the reader. Short of having access to the first several handwritten manuscripts, finding this "key" requires not just hyperattentive reading (both semantically and physiologically—can your eyes notice the spacing between *k* and *l* in *Entkleidung*?) of the *Letter* itself but an equally if not more attentive reading of both the *Golgotha* review and, even more radically, the *bordering* reviews closely enough to simply *notice* the change of "**Auf**klärung und Ent**sch**eidung" to "**Ver**klärung und Ent**k**leidung." But even assuming the reader has been able to pull off "the beard of my key" (R 29, 21)—a *disrobing* of the text's *disguise*—she is simply left standing before a "door and lock" (ibid.) with the task of unraveling the "typical meaning" of this citational trans- or disfiguration.[5]

5    It is important to note here that this project was explicitly conceived with a *public* audience in mind and not as a private game among friends who happen to subscribe to the *Allgemeine deutsche Bibliothek*. Hamann writes e.g. to Buchholtz: "To appeal to the public was the initial impetus and drive of my latest authorship, and I cannot deny this initial impulse" (July 17, 1786, ZH 997). In early March—before the commission of this critical crime—he provides Jacobi with a long list of names scattered across the German-speaking world to whom he would like to send copies of the first print run, prefaced by the statement: "Gegen 100 Exempl. denke *selbst* zu brauchen" (March 4/6, 1785, ZH 939, emphasis mine). Jacobi indeed printed 100 copies of the first almost-finished proof. In his first mention of the project to his frequent correspondent Herder, he writes: "Ich denke auch an meine Abschieds Audienz von Niemand dem Kundbaren" (December 13, 1775, ZH 905), and after Hamann gives up on the increasingly exhausting task of finishing the project, Herder writes: "Was macht Ihre Schrift? ... Sie haben die Hand einmal an den Pflug gelegt, ziehen Sie

The change remains through the end of the project, in all drafts; it survives numerous substantial deletions in the rewrite. There, in the second phase of the project (Nadler's "Second Version"), he insists upon this alteration with emphatic dots, one for each changed letter, a form of emphasis not present anywhere else in the available manuscripts:

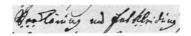

Figure 7: Universitäts- und Landesbibliothek Münster, N. Hamann, 1,47–4 (= R 37, 1vu).

The centrality of the review is also made more explicit in a reformulation of the call for the reader to take up the "gentle yoke" of opening up the *Universal German Library* and reading the review:

> Mit desto mehr Fuge darf ich dem freÿwilligen Leser das sanftene Joch auflegen, die seit langen Monaten auf meinem Pulte ruhende dreÿfältige Recension – ist sie doch klein und macht im ganzen XII Blätter aus! – als den Grundtext zu meinen Randgloßen, eigenhändig nachzuschlagen; weil kein Parallelismus ohne relative Vergleichung erkannt werden kann, jede Antwort und Auflösung in den Bedingungen ihrer vorausgesetzten Frage oder Aufgabe gegründet, und nach dem vielseitigen Sinn eines Knotens auch die Entwicklung deßelben erörtert werden muß. (38, 1r)

I am thus all the more justified in laying upon the voluntary reader the gentle yoke of personally consulting the threefold re-

nicht zurück … Es steht ja nachher bei Ihnen, ob Sie die Schrift publicieren wollen oder nicht" (January 1787, ZH 1042).

view which has been resting on my desk for long months – how small it is, though, made up of a total of XII pages! – as the original text to my marginal glosses; for no parallelism can be discerned without relative comparison, every answer and solution grounded in the conditions of their presupposed question or task, and the elaboration of the same must be argued according to the manifold sense of a knot.

This is one of Hamann's clearest formulations of his collisional theory of language, writing, and reading—an expression of his linguistic and intellectual anti-purism, most forcefully and famously expressed in his *Metacritique on the Purism of Reason* (N III 281–289).

It also further and again destabilizes *any* reading of Hamann: to take his often highly quotable, aphoristic moments of clarity at their face is to forget that all readings and writings are, for Hamann, "glosses" and that the generation of concepts occurs in "*radii reflexi*" not "*directi*" (ZH 1058), in tangent lines and glancing blows. For Hamann, reading is writing is language; each implies each. The *Brief* and its composition are tightly and even totally *tied* to the physical book lying (actually or not) on his "desk"—the knotted thread traced above is what ties the two texts together, and a centrifugal and centripetal force that both draws them together and forces them away.

Texts are only generated in "collision cases" (W 306) with other texts. That Hamann chooses to *abschließen* (conclude or close, but also lock or seal) his "authorship" with a relatively short response to a half-hearted, somewhat careless review of his work is telling, an example of the simultaneous enacting and/or embodying of a theoretical conviction, a procedure inherent in the underlying conviction itself, that the sensual "clothing" of reason is inseparable from that reason itself.

This is also, though disguised with characteristic "crocodilian melancholy" (R 5, 5r), another expression of a fundamental violence suffusing the text, concerning as it does the violation of one text by another and (by Hamann's own account) of one author by another, and of the reader not least of all. Hamannian collisionality is emphatically *not* a soothing, therapeutic vision of mutually respectful "dialogue" between texts; one does not contaminate, disfigure, violate a dialogue partner's language (and thus body, self, identity), seek in "agon" (W 314) for a dialogue partner to be destroyed. It is more analogous to the collision of physical bodies in space and, as we saw when Hamann assumed the Leibniz disguise, subject to similar laws. The texts themselves are bodies (physiological and physical) with their own agency; this is reinforced in the letters, where Hamann repeatedly reports of his inability to read his own text, to get it back under his control, to regain entry (to "find the thread again"). He writes repeatedly of the *Letter* as a "machine" with "organs"—terms he also uses to refer to himself writing, his own body-at-work and cognition. Any potential response to or unravelling of (at least; especially…) a Hamann text lies in exposure to the force or agency of the colliding text—whether the immediate, proximate text (here the Eberhardt reviews) or those innumerable "remote references" lying in wait in the rococo labyrinth of Hamann's vast referential and citational apparatus. Nor is there any reassuring notion of "encounter" here—rarely in space do physical bodies of equal resilience collide; not all things are equally elastic; some shatter; most shatter.

This disquieting element of "relative comparison" in Hamann is a poetics of collision and contamination highlighting the destructive potential of comparison, relationality, maybe of the very premise of philology, criticism, and "comparative literature." Attempting to untangle Hamann's many knots is something like accidentally stepping into a referential *Fastnacht* parade,[6] losing track of the distinction between scholarship and specter, or the presence of some other disorienting force.

---

6    "Fastnacht" (Allemanic Carneval) was a favorite trope of Hamann's, showing up e.g. on the cover of *An die Hexe zu Kadmonbor*, a wild text recording a conversation between Friedrich Nicolai and a witch. The publishing information is recorded as "Berlin. Geschrieben in der jungen Fastnacht."

## 6. The Skein of Immanence: Virtual Power, or Two Kinds of Nomad

> SKEIN. *n. ſ.* [*eſcaigne*, French.] A knot of thread or ſilk wound and doubled.
>
> Why art thou then exaſperate, thou idle immaterial *ſkein* of ſley'd ſilk, thou taſſel of a prodigal's purſe? *Shakeſp.*
>
> Our ſtile ſhould be like a *ſkein* of ſilk, to be found by the right thread, not ravell'd or perplexed. Then all is a knot, a heap. *Ben. Johnſon.*
>
> Beſides, ſo lazy a brain as mine is, grows ſoon weary when it has ſo entangled a *ſkein* as this to unwind. *Digby.*

A single thread, wound and doubled and raveled: how far is it from one end of this thread to the other? What is the length of a knot? Do we measure the length of a knotted thread from end to end along its entire body or do we measure the immediate interior distance from one end (as point) to the other end (as point)? What are the spatial dimensions of a Hamann text, or of fiction generally? How far is Thebes from Athens when travel between them is "instantaneous and irresistible"? Theseus walked between them, in an arc on land, along the coast. It took some time.

On the cover of this book you will see a mask. This mask, made of finely-hammered bronze and dating to the early 1st century BC, depicts the face of one of the most cryptic personalities of Greek myth, and a central figure of Greek theater: Silenus, the foster-father, teacher, and ever-drunken donkey-riding companion of Dionysus, god of wine. This particular mask, according to archaeologist Eugenio La Rocca, was most likely not worn by an actor but rather designed to be hung between two pillars amid a wreath of ivy as decoration in a Roman villa, or possibly placed over the face of a statue (held in place by loops of ribbon over the ears, threaded through the two small holes in the ears on either side of the mask).[1] It was crafted in a world not unlike the one covered in ash for nearly two millennia by Mount Vesuvius a hundred or so years later, a world become visible again with the excavation of the Villa of the Mysteries in Pompeii, the walls of which depict one woman's frightening initiation into the Bacchic mysteries, her encounters with the maenads and satyrs, with Bacchus, Silenus, and Pan—the Dionysian trinity. Like the Pompeii frescoes, the mask you see on the cover also lay forgotten for millennia, although not under ash but water: discovered at sea several decades ago, it was first exhibited to the public in Rome in 2010.

By the time some now-nameless bronzeworker crafted this mask, the cult of Dionysus (a god with many other names[2]) had already been repressed in Rome: the decree banning the Bacchanalia had been promulgated a century earlier, in 186 BC,[3] forcing the cult further underground, to become doubly

1    For a detailed analysis of the mask and its history, one of only two known bronze Silenus masks in the world, see: Eugenio La Rocca, "Vivere serenamente all'ombra di Dionisio: La maschera in bronzo die Papposileno della Fondazione Sorgente Group e la di svago nelle ville romane," *Il sorriso di Dioniso/The Smile of Dionysus* (Turin, New York, and Rome: Umberto Allemandi, 2010), p. 127–173.
2    Hamann's uncle Johann Georg (or George) Hamann the Older (1697–1733) in his *Poetisches Lexikon* lists Laius, Evan, Nomius, Liber, Iacchus, and Triambus as some alternative names. Johann George Hamann, *Poetisches Lexikon* (Leipzig, in der Großischen Handlung, 1751), p. 214.
3    P. G. Walsh, "Making a Drama out of a Crisis: Livy on the Bacchanalia," *Greece & Rome* 43/2 (1996): p. 188–203. Livy's sensationalist account of the claims which led to the ban is our best historical source, although it strongly resembles a form of public panic or mass hysteria which we are still familiar with to the present day: "the festival had earlier been confined to women, but in the grove of Stimula young men were being initiated into the cult, and there were allegations of both heterosexual and homosexual license. Though previously restricted to three days a year, the ceremonies were now being conducted five times a month; moreover, the proceedings were being held in darkness. Allegations of dire misconduct were circulat-

secret, doubly concealed. Their rites, by design and necessity secret from the start, were forced to further mask, disguise, and conceal themselves.

In masking itself, the cult of Dionysus became, in a sense, the cult of Silenus, whose cryptic, wine-soaked utterances were the epitome of ambiguity: a face grotesquely contorted into a threatening smile and ludicrous frown at once, a figure whose comic bearing, tottering and lolling atop his donkey, and incomprehensible utterances resolve, in many tellings, into their unsettling, tragic, life-regretting opposites.[4] Or sometimes the opposite: the undesirable Silenus becomes the desired, e.g. in Euripides' raucous and peculiar satyr play *Cyclops*. There, the old, ugly Silenus is transfigured, with the help of a great deal of wine, into a beautiful Ganymede and taken to bed by the Cyclops Polyphemus. After that, Odysseus blinds Polyphemus and leads away his freed slaves—the satyrs—to become (again) the willing slaves of Dionysus.

Much later, around Christmas of 1759, a twenty-nine-year-old Hamann wrote a letter to his friend Immanuel Kant, who was trying to recruit him to participate in a project inspired by Diderot's and d'Alembert's still-in-progress *Encyclopédie*, which was at the time about halfway finished. Hamann, "for the boredom of the public by a lover of boredom,"[5] had just

ing, including charges of murder of unwilling initiates, forging of the wills of the dead, and perjury" (ibid., p. 188).

4    Plutarch quoting a lost work of Aristotle (*Eudemus*) in *Moralia*: "But for men it is utterly impossible that they should obtain the best thing of all, or even have any share in its nature (for the best thing for all men and women is not to be born); however, the next best thing to this, and the first of those to which man can attain, but nevertheless only the second best, is, after being born, to die as quickly as possible." Plutarch, "A Letter of Condolence to Apollonius," *Moralia*, vol. 2, trans. Frank Cole Babbitt (Cambridge, Mass. and London: Harvard University Press), p. 179.

5    The subtitle of *Socratic Memorabilia*.

published *Socratic Memorabilia*. Apart from the dedication to our by-now familiar acquaintance Nobody, the Well-known, Hamann later appended[6] a citation from Euripides' *Cyclops*: "NOBODY, where is he?"[7] The letter contains the first epigraph to the book you are now reading, which in more context reads:

> Always see my *parrhesia* as the sacrilege of a *homeromastix* or as a cynical impertinence. You are free to give things names as you please – – Not your language, not mine, not your reason, not mine: here it is clock versus clock. But the sun alone runs true; and if even it does not run true it is still its shadow at noon which distributes time past all dispute.[8]
>
> If you want to be a learned conqueror like Bacchus then you would do well to choose a Silenus for your companion. I do not love wine for wine's sake but because it gives me a tongue to tell you the truth in my stupor on the back of my donkey.

6    Krauss, "Hamann's Latent Parrhesia," p. 65. Nadler took the liberty of inserting this later addition without comment into the main text in his edition.

7    The words of the Cyclops after being blinded by Odysseus, and a play on words: Odysseus had told Polyphemus that his name was "Nobody" (*Cyclops* 9.366).

8    The German phrasing has a curious babbling quality, and plays with conjunctions in a way hard to replicate in English: "Die Sonne aber geht allein recht; und wenn sie auch nicht recht geht, so ist es doch ihr Mittagsschatten allein, der die Zeit über allen Streit eintheilt." This ceased being true with the assignment of the prime meridian in the 19th century: time has become geodetic, a function of geographic meridians. Hamann's affinity with Kafka, Celan, Cormac MacCarthy, and Oswald Egger might have something to do with this interest in geodesy.

> Because I esteem you highly, I am your Zoilus; and Diogenes pleased a certain man who shared with him the same inclinations; however dissimilar the roles they played were.[9]

Kant as Bacchus, erudite conqueror? And the Kant of 1759 at that, which is to say a Kant still very much dogmatically aslumber:[10] the first *Critique* will not be published for another twenty-two years. This is the Kant of that elusive persona traced (just as elusively) by Jean-Luc Nancy in *The Discourse of the Syncope*:[11] the ambitious, talented, effortlessly elegant prose stylist who transforms, somehow, and somehow willingly, into a generator of dark, difficult, obscure sentences—their obscurity being somehow linked to the alleged clarity of the thoughts underneath them. Hamann, in contrast, springs from the head of Zeus fully formed: the Hamann we hear in this letter is more or less the same Hamann we hear more than twenty-five years later.

This book's second epigraph is taken from another work that marked a shift from effortless narrative clarity to chiaroscuro theoretical theater: Gilles Deleuze's *Difference and Repetition*. After a decade of publishing a series of stud-

---

9   *Parrhesia* is free and frank speech; the *homeromastix*, "scourge of Homer," is the Cynic Zoilus (ca. 400–320 BC) who wrote invectives against Homer, Plato, and Isocrates; the "certain man" is Alexander the Great, who admired the contrarian Cynic Diogenes and died in Babylon as a dissolute drunk, possibly poisoned, having taken his Dionysian devotions rather too seriously. For more on Hamann's understanding of *parrhesia* in light of Foucault's reading of the concept, see Andrea Krauss, "Hamann's Latent Parrhesia," p. 76–80.

10   A slumber likely broken by Hamann, one of the earliest enthusiastic readers of Hume in the German-speaking world. He translated Hume into German and introduced Kant to a number of his texts.

11   Jean-Luc Nancy, *The Discourse of the Syncope: Logodaedalus* (Stanford: Stanford University Press, 2008).

ies in the history of philosophy—of Spinoza, Hume, Kant, Nietzsche, Bergson, and Proust, all written in an elegant, readable, reportative style—Deleuze published the "first book in which I try to 'do philosophy.'"[12] It is a task framed from the start in terms of theater, drama, and the mask, building on "a force common to Kierkegaard and Nietzsche"[13] each of whom "in his own way, makes repetition not only a power peculiar to language and thought, a superior pathos and pathology, but also the fundamental category of a philosophy of the future. To each corresponds a Testament as well as a Theatre."[14] Their joint aim, in Deleuze's account, is to bypass accounting (representation) to operate in the realm of movement (repetition):

> They want to put metaphysics in motion, in action. They want to make it act, and make it carry out immediate acts. It is not enough, therefore, for them to propose a new representation of movement; representation is already mediation. Rather, it is a question of producing within the work a movement capable of affecting the mind outside of all representation. ... [Kierkegaard's] "I only look at the movements" is the language of a director who poses the highest theatrical problem, the problems of a movement which would directly touch the soul, which would be that of the soul.[15]

The deeper target, then, is mediation itself. Deleuze positions himself above all against Hegel, the Great Mediator who

12    Gilles Deleuze, *Difference and Repetition*, trans. Paul Patton (New York: Columbia University Press, 1994), p. xv.
13    Ibid., p. 5.
14    Ibid.
15    Ibid., p. 8–9.

"represents concepts instead of dramatizing ideas: he creates a false theatre, a false drama, a false movement."[16] Deleuze's complaint has, interestingly, little or nothing to do with any of Hegel's propositions or concepts per se but rather with his failure to properly *stage* or *dramatize* these concepts, which would lend them the *immediacy* and *presence* through which ideas first *become* ideas.

Deleuze, in contrast, seeks out a theoretical space which is also a "theatrical space, the emptiness of that space, and the manner in which it is filled and determined by the signs and masks through which an actor plays a role *which plays other roles*."[17] Theory is a role within a role and a mask over a mask:

> Remember the song of Ariadne from the mouth of the old Sorcerer: here, two masks are superimposed – that of a young woman, almost of a *Kōre*, which has just been laid over the mask of a repugnant old man. The actor must play the role of an old man playing the role of a *Kōre*. Here, too, for Nietzsche, it is a matter of filling the inner emptiness of the mask within a theatrical space: by multiplying the superimposed masks and inscribing the omnipresence of Dionysus in that superimposition[.][18]

In his 1970 review of this work (along with *The Logic of Sense*) under the title "Theatrum Philosophicum," Foucault recognizes this theatrical, Dionysian dimension to Deleuze's thought, which he links to Deleuze's stance towards Plato. He poses a question which answers itself: "Are all philosophies individual species of the genus 'anti-Platonic'? Would each

---

16    Ibid., p. 10.
17    Ibid., emphasis Deleuze's.
18    Ibid.

begin with a declaration of this fundamental rejection?"[19] What makes Deleuze stand out in the pantheon of mid-century French theorists is precisely this unabashed embrasure of capital-P Philosophy, which is and always has been Metaphysics, through what Foucault terms a form of "reverse Platonism."

Deleuze joins Alcibiades, Hamann, and Nietzsche in affirming the fundamentally dithyrambic, Dionysian, and satyric nature of philosophy: "Opposed to the clear-and-distinct of Apollonian representation, Ideas are Dionysian, existing in an obscure zone which they themselves preserve and maintain ... the obscure zone of an intoxication which will never be calmed; the distinct–obscure as the double colour with which philosophy paints the world, with all the forces of a differential unconscious."[20]

The double-colored field of movement between the distinct and obscure, between light and darkness, between presence and absence is the domain of the virtual, which is always a double domain: first in the general question of how perception of the absent (in memory, fantasy, dream, etc.—what is a dragon?) is possible in the first place; and then in the specific dynamics of this field: where are your memories when you are not remembering them? Your dreams when you are not dreaming them? Where are Rosencrantz and Guildenstern? With Hamlet?

Deleuze, building on Bergson, links the virtual above all to memory: "The virtual is not opposed to the real but to the actual. *The virtual is fully real in so far as it is virtual.* Exactly

19    Michel Foucault, *Aesthetics, Method, and Epistemology*, ed. James D. Faubion, trans. Robert Hurley and others (New York: The New Press, 1998), p. 344.
20    Deleuze, *Difference and Repetition*, p. 280.

what Proust said of states of resonance must be said of the virtual: 'Real without being actual, ideal without being abstract'; and symbolic without being fictional."[21] A philosophy of the virtual is an immensely positive philosophy, dispensing with concern for Nothing and the Other, an affirmation that *nothing can be anything other than something*.

Hamann more resolutely emphasizes the role of the future, through the vehicles of fiction and prophecy:

> The spirit of observation and the spirit of prophecy are the wings of human genius [*Genius*]. To the sphere of the former belongs everything present; to the sphere of the latter everything absent, of past and future. The philosophical genius [*Genie*] expresses its power in endeavoring, by means of abstraction, to make the present absent, to *disrobe* actual [*wirkliche*] objects into naked concepts and merely thinkable characteristics, into pure appearances and phenomena. The poetic genius [*Genie*] expresses its power in *transfiguring*, by means of fiction, visions of absent past and future into present representations [*Darstellungen*]. Criticism and politics *resist* the usurpations of both powers, and ensure balance between them, through these same positive forces [*Kräfte*] and means of observation and prophecy. (W 334, emphasis mine)

The immediate purpose of this model in the *Letter* is to serve as scaffolding for a prophetic, apocalyptic reading of Mendelssohn's title, *Jerusalem*—generating a theory which then gains immediate enactment. Examining the swerves and tangles of that reading unfortunately goes beyond the bounds of this book, but the critical point to recognize is the collisional

---

21    Ibid., emphasis Deleuze's.

character of this theory, informed by Hamann's passionate (but qualified) Humean empiricism: concepts and theories are useful tools in concrete situations, determined by their concrete relations in a specific historical moment. Hamann, though, does not *dispose* of his theoretical apparatus once its function has been served, as a thoroughgoing empiricist might; instead—and maybe we could venture to call him here a "transcendental empiricist"—he maintains it but (re-)virtualizes it. It is *real* but—and this is written into the theory itself—fluctuates between actuality and non-actuality, function and non-function.

This theory is a *virtual theory* in that it hangs suspended, fully real and capable of effect if brought back onto the stage of attention but simply *absent* for the moment, non-actual, in a space not unlike the one where that memory of that time your mother forgot hangs suspended, or the name Flacius Fulbert, or that photograph you are pretty sure you deleted and sincerely hope is forever irretrievable. (As we all slowly learn how permanently retrievable our lives and histories in fact are, digitally and otherwise, the stakes of a meaningful theory of the virtual become ever clearer.)

In the following paragraph, all of the above resolves into the "many-headed modifications" of drive and desire:

> The present is an indivisible, simple point into which the spirit of observation concentrates itself [*in den sich der Geist der Beobachtung concentriert*], and from it has an effect on the entire sphere of the general faculty of cognition [*Erkenntnisvermögen*]. The absent has a double dimension, can be divided into past and future in line with the equally ambiguous spirit of prophecy ... Because, then, the sum of the present is infinitely small as compared to the manifold aggregate of the absent, and the spirit of prophecy infinitely superior to the simple spirit of observation, so is our

faculty of cognition dependent on the many-headed modifications of the most intimate, darkest, and deepest drives of desire and consent, to which it must be subject. (W 334)

This passage is expanded upon greatly in a handwritten manuscript page, which no one to my knowledge has yet written about. It is the only remaining of a total three draft pages, the other two being lost or destroyed. It deserves to be quoted in full, and its significance—both in the history of thought and for our own theories of language and the virtual today—largely speaks for itself:

### No. III

Even mathematical certainty seems to rest more on good will than on the healthy concepts of our scholastic logic. Archimedes' presumptuous postulate for the miracle of his boastful machine was a pure impossibility, and the first-order element for his entire theory of quantity is, like the "keystone of the free-floating vault of heaven and earth," a *pure word* in its most fundamental sense, just as much as a physical nothing or an object of natural absence. Thus, even though I compared the present with an indivisible point, the term consists in an empty philosophical abstraction and vain poetic fiction, whose literal expression and figural name must, *cum grano salis*, be taken and interpreted diacritically and metapolitically, which is to say *intellectualiter*, *virtualiter*, *potentialiter*, or spiritually [*geistlich*].

But just as presence and absence are nothing more than predicates of a single positive thing, so too are the spirit of observation and prophecy expressions of a single positive force, which can naturally be separated as little from the subject as from the object of this force, but instead always presuppose each other, or relate to each other.

All relative terms are thus only thinkable, and have no other reality than that inherent in their signs, which are really nothing less than what they represent and signify, but are instead simply subjective conditionals and aids in the designation and definition of predicates, which relate both not to the properties of the object and instead to our knowledge of the same.

Hence, reason is jointly impregnated and made fruitful through language, or conversely this one through that one, by the spirit of observation and of prophecy. From one side, criticism and politics are the guardians and pedagogues: from the other side they could, as already happened above, be called diacriticism and metapolitics – – – *si forte necesse est*

*Jndiciis monstrare recentibus*
*abdita rerum.*

An impure, mixed mother tongue corresponds to the *orignibus* and *Initiis* of philosophy, which is documentably a barbaric graft on a wild trunk, and through our culture seems to be returning to its original nature, the restoration of which might require yet another barbarity, which the evening redness of our latest ~~barbarians~~ Enlightenment seems to be a harbinger of.

The present thus relates, its indivisibility notwithstanding, to the past as effect and with the future as cause — (R 16, 3r-3v, emphasis Hamann's)

We can—in a fully "diacritical" spirit, with a grain of salt, a yes-and-no—distill a number of propositions here:

1.  Even mathematics is rendered impure by the original sin of Archimedes' "presumptuous postulate," i.e. the Archimedean point: an idealized point of perspective completely apart from and thus not entangled in the observed system. (Keywords: *perspectivism*, *relativity*, *observer effect*.)

2. There is no text but context, words only relate, a "pure word" or word out of context (as in a definition, or as an object of mystical contemplation) is like a keystone without an arch. There is no physics of nothing (and hence, perhaps, no nothing) as there are no "naturally absent" objects, just objects which, right now, happen to be elsewhere. (*Relativism, deixis, positivity.*)

3. My own propositions are mental constructions which serve a certain function in a certain relative context. Positing the potential tends to unavoidably effect a certain self-actuation. The proposition is not recanted or negated; it's both true and not, it remains in effect somewhere, elsewhere, it is as real as fiction is real. (*Nominalism, pragmatism, positing*, Setzung.)

4. "Intellectually," "virtually," and "potentially" are synonyms. (*Virtuality, power, thought.*)

5. Signs are relative and nothing *less* (!) than what they signify. They are as real as fiction is real. (*Semiotics, paradox.*)

6. All of this, and all words, and everything else really, is, anyways, simply *the expression of a single positive force.* Thought and language—and especially "reason"—trail or express desires, drives, affects. (*The unconscious, will-to-power.*)

7. (Dia-)criticism and (meta-)politics both serve special functions in this regime, somehow counteracting or guiding the dynamics of presence and desire. (*Political theology, metacriticism.*)

8. Enlightenment pretends to have transcended its barbaric origins, which means that it will one day, and probably soon, bring about some new monstrous act of barbarity, precisely through refusing to recognize its own enmeshment in the dynamics of desire, which are inescapable. (*Dialectics of Enlightenment.*)

It is the sheer density of prior convergence with later thought that makes Hamann somehow perennially inexplicable; and when he lets his mask slip, we encounter a lucid, clear, and direct writer—a philosopher even. Any one or two of these threads taken alone or together eventually became schools of later thought in the 20th century. It really is no exaggeration to say that their simultaneous presence on a single manuscript page in 1786 is astonishing.

Of these many threads, I want to draw particular attention to the conjunction of *virtualiter*, *potentialiter*, and *intellectualiter*, which should be read together with the notion of *expressions of a single positive force*. Hamann's listing of these words together as effective equivalents is on one level an expression of his nominalism, his disdain for definition and "scholasticism," and an affirmation of the context-dependence of words. The next-level and maybe more interesting question is *why* these words are classed together. Charles Peirce at least, citing Duns Scotus, sees *potential* as "almost [the] contrary" of *virtual*, in that "the potential X is of the nature of X, but is without actual efficiency."[22]

*Virtual* is one of those words only comprehensible through a double or opposite: what is the mirror, double, or contrary of "virtual"? Is it *actual*, as Deleuze maintains, or *potential* as Charles Peirce suggests, or something else entirely?

**Real Presence: Flacius Fulbert Pt. II**

In 1079, the year Fulbert's eventual victim Peter Abelard was born, another stubbornly controversial monk by the name of

22  Charles S. Peirce, "Virtual," *Dictionary of Philosophy and Psychology*, vol. 2 (London: Macmillan, 1902), p. 763–764.

Berengar of Tours (c. 999–1088) was forced to sign the last of many statements rejecting his former, now officially heretical teachings on the nature of the Eucharist. The doctrine which he held to over decades, recanting only when politically necessary, was that Jesus Christ was only virtually (*virtualiter*) present in the Eucharist and not bodily (*corporaliter*).[23] This is if not the first then certainly among the earliest attestations of the word *virtualis* and its variants, derived from Berengar's defense of an earlier thinker, Ratramnus, also condemned for claiming that Christ was not in the Eucharist *in veritate* but *in figura*, *in mysterio*, *in virtute*: not *in truth* but in *form*, in *mystery*, in *power*.[24]

Both terms were in turn rooted in Latin *virtus*, a word combining *vir-* (man) and *-tus* (-ness) into something similar to "maleness" in English, with an associated collection of figurative meanings in classical Latin ranging from "virility" and "strength" to "excellence" and "virtue." The transformation of the term by 1046, when Berengar was first condemned for using it in an intellectual sense, is a neat and concrete reflection of a shift in ethics and morality brought by Christianity

23    Alois Knöpfler, *Lehrbuch der Kirchengeschichte* (Freiburg im Breisgau: Herder, 1895), p. 288. Interestingly, Oswald Spengler cites this specific controversy as the intellectual origin of "Faustian"—i.e. Western European—philosophy and religion. In: *Der Untergang des Abendlandes: Umrisse einer Morphologie der Weltgeschichte* [1923] (Munich: DTV, 1972), p. 237–238. The word would again ignite controversy when Luther and Zwingli (the latter a virtualist) debated the nature of the Eucharist.

24    The only extant copy of this manuscript was discovered by Lessing in the Wolfenbüttel library in 1770, after which he published a short introduction to the work and its author entitled *Berengarius Turonensis* (Braunschweig, am Verlage der Buchhandlung des Waisenhauses, 1770). Matthias Flacius also makes an appearance in Lessing's text: "The writings of Berengarius must have as good as vanished from the world by the time of Flacius" whose "*improbus labor* [measureless efforts] in every sense of the word" as a scholar and manuscript collector were legendary (p. 6).

as later famously condemned by Nietzsche in his *Genealogy of Morals*: no longer simply a function of strength, excellence, or raw power, morals had become *mediated* and lost their connection to figure, shape, and appearance. This was not an abstract type of mediation, either: it was about the power and authority (*exousia*)[25] of the priesthood and their regime of censorship.

I find this early distinction useful: at its origins the virtuality dispute was not primarily about "reality," "potentiality," or "actuality"—no one doubted (publicly) whether Christ was *really* present in the bread and the wine, only what the *character* of (this) reality was: what kind of reality do signs and symbols have as compared to bodies? How intimate a relationship is there between signifier and signified? What is the nature of representation? Or even: what is *more real*, sign, symbol, and figure, or body and matter? (This is still in terms of concrete sensual signs—bread, wine—not yet writing and language.) Was God's *body* present in the Eucharist or did it *act* in his stead, as his *agent*? This is a debate flowing from pre-Nicene questions (taken up again shortly thereafter in Islam) about whether Jesus of Nazareth was God himself or simply an agent of God. Separated from its specific theological concerns, it is also the beginning of a conversation about action-at-a-distance, the conveyance of authority, and the power and authority of the priesthood—both a literal institutional priesthood and the various organs of mediation which anarchic thinkers like Nietzsche and Deleuze would later take as their target.

---

25  *Exousia*, cited by Hamann in the veil/power paragraph above, is among the more cryptic words in the New Testament, but is generally used to refer to *absolute* power (see Matthew 28:18, John 17:2, John 19). It is a power which Jesus conveys to Paul and the Apostles to act in his name, which thus, in the reading still held to by the Roman Catholic Church, conveys absolute authority to the Church and all of its priests.

**If Socrates could write…**

"Repetition is the power of language."[26] What must it have been like for Socrates or Plato or Alcibiades to hear the initiates begin their hypnotic procession from Athens to Eleusis on the sixth day of the mysteries?—The rhythmic smash of cymbals, beat of drums, blaring of horns, shouts lolled out treading the lines between cry, song, and speech?—Repeated shouts of *Iakkhos! Iakkhos!* where name meets nonsense and exclamation? Was it more like the wild revelries you will hear to this day on Easter Eve in Naples, the all-night city-wide marches and musicmaking (water-sober though, somber in frenzy, processants pious and barefaced under the images of the Virgin borne aloft on their shoulders)? Or was it more like the final nights of *Fastnacht*, forty days before and seven degrees more north, with its pageants of grotesque and ridiculous masks, shapes in costume in marchstep yet each somehow released to themselves as rhythmant figure solitary, cutting clothes in ritual (fringe for Pappageno, scissors for fathers' ties), forbidden brushes with strangers in delirious drunken crowds, cries of *Ho Narro!* or *Hi Ha Ho!* or *Bitzi, batzi!*?[27] Was Bacchus just a cry given a name which took on the body of a god?

Plato, it is said, began his career writing dithyrambs, lyrics, and tragedies[28]—and was thus perhaps a leader of one of

26   Deleuze, *Difference and Repetition*, p. 291.
27   As Horace knew, and I learned when living in Constance, the best place to spend Saturnalia is as far from the city and its revelries as possible: even if you do manage to fall asleep, you'll be startled awake at six in the morning by schoolchildren ringing your doorbell. The specific *Narrenrufe* or fools' calls belong, respectively, to Constance, Hard (Austria), and Triesenberg (Liechtenstein).
28   Diogenes Laertius, *Lives of Eminent Philosophers*, vol. III: *Plato*, ed. Jeffrey Henderson, trans. R.D. Hicks (Cambridge, Mass.: Harvard Univer-

these processions, thyrsus low then aloft then low in cadent rhythm. Only a chance meeting with Socrates in an alleyway—where Socrates thrust out his walking stick and asked Plato where to find some food, and then where to find where "men become good and honorable"[29]—caused him to burn his poems and plays and become a disciple of the impious sophist. He apparently could not help himself, and returned to the genre, giving us Philosophy.[30]

To return to the problem (exaggeratedly generalizing, but usefully so) posed by Foucault: if the problem of philosophy is, finally, the problem of Plato, then Hamann and Deleuze

---

sity Press, 1972): "He was taught letters in the school of Dionysius, who is mentioned by him in the *Rivals*. And he learnt gymnastics under Ariston, the Argive wrestler. And from him he received the name of Plato on account of his *robust figure* ... But others affirm that he got the name Plato from the *breadth of his style*, or from the *breadth of his forehead*, as suggested by Neanthes. Others again affirm that he wrestled in the Isthmian Games—this is stated by Dicaearchus in his first book *On Lives*—and *that he applied himself to painting and wrote poems, first dithyrambs, afterwards lyric poems and tragedies*. He had, they say, a weak voice; this is confirmed by Timotheus the Athenian in his book *On Lives*. It is stated that Socrates in a dream saw a cygnet on his knees, which all at once put forth plumage, and flew away after uttering a loud sweet note. And the next day Plato was introduced as a pupil, and thereupon he recognized in him the swan of his dream ... Afterwards, when he was about to compete for the prize with a tragedy, he listened to Socrates in front of the theatre of Dionysus, and then consigned his poems to the flames, with the words:
 *Come hither, O fire-god, Plato now has need of thee.*
From that time onward, having reached his twentieth year (so it is said), he was the pupil of Socrates" (p. 279–281).

29   Actually Xenophon's first encounter with Socrates, but likely to be as true (or not) of either. (Diog. Laert. 2.6.48.)

30   Socrates and Euripides were, in Diogenes' telling, both pupils of Anaxagoras (Diog. Laert. 2.5.45), who, like Socrates later, was charged with impiety, then banished from Athens. Euripides was only much later charged with impiety by Nietzsche, for sacrilege against Dionysus—by Socratizing theater.

present (to myself usefully exaggerate) the only two routes out: conscious complicity or dissident reaction, embrace or rebellion. Deleuze takes the former route, embracing Plato and his Ideas-in-Writing, and Hamann the latter, by taking Socrates seriously for once: smuggling the critique of writing *into* writing by forcing writing to its limits, tying it in knots, bending it, nagging it, entangling it into little less than a "convulsive gesture" (W 333) on the page.

Ambiguity belongs to writing more than to speech: the *langage* of tone and situation, operating more in the register of the phrase than the word or sentence, provides little time or space for doubt. Accomplishing ambiguity in speech is in fact a feat that seems to provoke its own transcription: is it possible that people chose to write down the ambiguous parables of e.g. Jesus or Zen masters *because* of their ambiguity, *because* of their incomprehensibility? This seems to be a function of time: a paradox or parable, admitting of multiple meanings, requires time to study. Socrates' main concern about writing seemed to relate to its deleterious effect on memory:[31] this might be true of the recording of unambiguous facts but fails when confronted with the parable or riddle: they would be forgotten if not written down.

Where Hamann and Deleuze most severely diverge is in their approach to the question of immanence. Both deny—or commit their work to undermining the idea of—a real difference between the immanent and transcendent, "phenomenon" and "noumenon," "subject" and "object," "self" and "other," or whatever other names you prefer. Hamann has long been read as performing this (primarily, or even exclusively) in the name of religion and faith, but this argument

---

31    Cf. *Phaedrus* 275.

becomes (to repeat...) even more tenuous, or simply misses the mark in light of comments like the following, written to Jacobi after receiving Jacobi's newest work, showing how closely together lie thought and disdain, honesty and cruelty:

> Forgive my vanity when I honestly admit that my own authorship is more plausible than yours, and even seems more important and useful in intent and content. Idealism and realism are nothing more than *entia rationis*, waxen noses – Christianity and Lutheranism are *res facti*, living organs and tools... (ZH 1058)

> Being, faith, reason are all simply relations that cannot be treated of absolutely, are not things but simple scholastic terms, signs to understand not to admire, aids in stimulating our attention, not shackling it ... Your theory is a truly botched patchwork of philosophical and human authorities – do you not feel that, dear Jonathan[?] (ZH 1060)

Hamann is indeed attempting to save something: the body and its language. That, perhaps, is his greatest sacrilege: instrumentalizing the divine. Faced with the dying or dead vocabulary of Christianity, Hamann was correct in his self-estimate in these letters: while Jacobi was attempting to erect a sanctuary around his inherited faith, Hamann was burning down the temple by transferring the language of the divine into *the language of the body* and *the body of language*. Did Hamann realize he was the first authentic atheist?

This is an intellectual history running through the first philosopher to firmly decouple the concept of the virtual from the Eucharist, and another in the line of censored dissident scholastics repeatedly invoked by Hamann: Duns Scotus (1266–1308). Duns Scotus is the thinker of univocity, and as such, in Deleuze's account, the intellectual progenitor of his own (and Spinoza's) brand of immanentism; the intellectual framework for the concept of difference in *Difference and Repetition* is developed in conversation with Duns Scotus' account of genus, species, and specific and generic difference. "There has only ever been one ontological proposition: Being is univocal. There has only ever been one ontology, that of Duns Scotus, which gave being a single voice."[32] The medieval dispute about univocity and equivocity, or realism and nominalism, was a dispute about the relationship(s) between and among words, ideas, and things, beginning with the words *God* and *being* (always the best test cases—might the battle already be lost in bringing God down as a theoretical *tool?*) and moving from there: when we say that God "is," is the sense of "is" being used the same as when we use it of "lily" or "dragonfly"? The *univocity of being* is the proposition that being—first as a word and then, on its own terms irresistibly, actually—has a single voice or sense: God *is* in the same sense that sun, lily, and dragonfly are.[33]

Here is where the *real* enters the scene. The discursive-analytical question of whether any given proposed difference is a *real* difference or only a *virtual* difference (or intellectual, or apparent—the "distinction without a difference") shifts in Duns Scotus into the proposition or observation that the sim-

---

32    Deleuze, *Difference and Repetition*, p. 36.

33    The dangerous consequence for the censors is, of course, that sun, lily, and dragonfly are just as divine as God (or, from another angle, that God is "only" as divine as sun, lily, and dragonfly), which means that sacraments, and thus the Church, are unnecessary, which means that no more mediators are required, which means that the priests and censors lose their jobs. Rabelais had considerable trouble with the censors. Maybe the most telling fact in this regard is that Rabelais' scatological parodies of the mass seemed to present few problems for the censors at the Sorbonne, while satire of those very same censors imperiled Rabelais and his book most of all.

ple fact *that* a difference has been posited is evidence enough for the reality of that difference. Reality, difference, and the virtual are thus subsumed to the same plane: the plane of immanence, which is the plane of the virtual. To posit is, irresistibly, to actuate, to suppose is to enact. The paradoxical and potentially problematic consequence of this is that in asserting the reality of any virtual difference, i.e. that the real is *constituted by* difference, even that the real *is* difference per se—at first glance a radical affirmation of the different, the multiple, the other, the diverse—might actually *negate* the different by relegating it to a homogenous immanent order of the same, though it happens to be named the different.

Maybe the greatest danger in Deleuze's understanding of the virtual and the immanent is precisely its planarity and linearity—rooted in a mathematical (Cartesian and then, especially, Leibnizian) model of space—with the attendant infinities and flatness and straightness, where even curvature becomes the product of an infinite series of straight lines (in calculus). The dangers of this flatness can be detected in the figures of the *plateau* and the *map*: flatness without infinity ends at a cliff, or an edge—or in a kind of mysticism detectable in his latest and earliest work, the mysterious "rips" or "holes" through which "an outside" might be glimpsed.[34] For Hamann there is no "outside"—making this adamant Lutheran less of a mystic than the atheist Deleuze. The history of figuration—in languages, types, signs, phenomena of experience, history, fiction, poetry, etc.—is revelation enough, more than enough. The paradoxical homogeneity and flatness of

34    Gilles Deleuze, "The Exhausted," trans. Anthony Uhlmann, *SubStance* 24/3 (1995): p. 3–28.

Deleuze's apparently hyper-heterogeneous oeuvre is the basis of the most convincing critiques of Deleuze.[35]

However tempted he may have been by flatness, Deleuze did not stay flat: there arrives suddenly his remarkable study of Leibniz, *The Fold,* in 1988. In this late (and once again solitary) return to the history of philosophy, Deleuze grapples with precisely the problem of how the plane with all of its flatness and homogeneity can generate difference. He does this through the vehicle of the Baroque: "The Baroque refers not to an essence but rather to an operative function, to a trait. It endlessly produces folds. It does not invent things ... the Baroque trait twists and turns its folds, pushing them to infinity, fold over fold, one upon the other."[36] It is also a study of labyrinths: "A labyrinth is said, etymologically, to be multiple because it contains many folds. The multiple is not only what has many parts but what is folded in many ways."[37] He engages with Leibniz by assuming Leibniz's language: "With Leibniz the curvature of the universe is prolonged according to three other fundamental notions: the fluidity of matter, the elasticity of bodies, and motivating spirit as a mechanism."[38] On the relation between "elastic" and "plastic" forces:

35   See e.g. Alain Badiou, *Deleuze: The Clamor of Being*, trans. Louise Burchill (Minneapolis: University of Minnesota Press, 1999) or Slavoj Žižek, *Organs without Bodies: On Deleuze and Consequences* (Abington and New York: Routledge, 2004). It is notable that both of these critiques were written by unabashed totalitarians: Badiou the Maoist reads Deleuze into a secret authoritarian, while Žižek helpfully informs us that Deleuze was always secretly an orthodox Hegelian anyways. Deleuze's work, like Hamann's, tends to provoke a greater-than-average degree of projection on the part of its readers.

36   Gilles Deleuze, *The Fold: Leibniz and the Baroque*, trans. Tom Conley (Minneapolis: University of Minnesota Press, 1993), p. 3.

37   Ibid.

38   Ibid., p. 4.

Whether organic or inorganic, matter is all one; but active forces are not the only ones exerted upon it … Material forces, which account for the organic fold, have only to be distinguished from the preceding forces, to transform raw matter into organic matter. In contrast to compressive or elastic forces, Leibniz calls them "plastic forces." They organize masses but, although the latter prepare organisms or make them possible by motivating drive, it is impossible to go from masses to organisms, since organs are always based on these plastic forces that preform them, and are distinguished from forces of mass, to the point where every organ is born from a preexisting organ.[39]

With the concept of the fold—of tissue, fabric, paper, to the two-dimensional surface—Deleuze seeks a solution to a problem, one he must have recognized: how do the planes of matter take on the curvature and color of being as we perceive it?

This planarity also extends to Deleuzian politics: the nomads of the "Treatise on Nomadology" in *A Thousand Plateaus*[40] operate in "smooth" spaces, barbarians sweeping across steppes and desert places on horseback with the bronze blades forged by their sacred metallurgists.[41] The year associated with the chapter is 1227, the year of Genghis Khan's death: Deleuze's barbarians arrive unexpectedly from a geographic exterior to the state, glide as a war machine through empty, flat spaces to smash the somnolent state from without, an abrupt awakening at once political and philosophical, the violent and sudden obliteration captured in *The Fold* in a strik-

---

39    Ibid., p. 7.
40    Gilles Deleuze and Félix Guattari, *A Thousand Plateaus: Capitalism and Schizophrenia*, trans. Brian Massumi (Minneapolis: University of Minnesota Press), p. 351–423
41    Ibid., p. 404–415.

ing quote from Thomas de Quincey's *Revolt of the Tartars*[42] about "the hallucinated gaze" confronted with "the event" of the last significant steppe migration in the 1770s.[43] Thomas de Quincey envisions the sleeping gaze of a Russian soldier confronted with the event of nomadic revolt:

> But sometimes, as the wind slackened or died away, all those openings, of whatever form, in the cloudy pall, would slowly close, and for a time the whole pageant was shut up from view; although the growing din, the clamors, the shrieks, and groans ascending from infuriated myriads, *reported, in a language not to be misunderstood*, what was going on behind the cloudy screen.[44]

Force, violence, panic, and pain constitute a language that escapes or resists the order of interpretation.[45] This is a function of immediacy and presence, the sharpening of attention and awareness.

42    "There is no great event in modern history, or, perhaps it may be said more broadly, none in all history, from its earliest records, less generally known, or more striking to the imagination, than the flight eastwards of a principal Tartar nation across the boundless steppes of Asia in the latter half of the last century" (Thomas de Quincy, *The Revolt of the Tartars*, in *Collected Writings*, vol. 7 [Edinburgh: Adam and Charles Black, 1890], p. 368–421). They were of course not boundless: the Kalyuks fled genocidal Russian persecution to arrive in China, where they were forced to permanently give up their nomadic way of life and become sedentary farmers.

43    Hamann, who lived during the period of the Kalyuk migration, also demonstrated an interest in the nomadic Tartars in his notebooks (N V 347).

44    de Quincy, *The Revolt of the Tartars*, p. 411–412, as cited in Deleuze, *The Fold*, p. 94, emphasis mine.

45    In J.M. Coetzee's *Waiting for the Barbarians*, the Magistrate arrives at the ironic dissolution and resolution of truth into power in recounting a discussion about torture as a method of truth-finding: "Pain is truth; all else is subject to doubt" (J.M. Coetzee, *Waiting for the Barbarians* [New York: Penguin Books, 1982], p. 6).

Hamann, too, as Carol Jacobs puts it, "is a nomadic writer. Just when you think you know where he is, just when you hear a voice beckoning you to 'turn aside,' and stay a while, it turns out he has pulled up stakes and pitched his tent elsewhere."[46] Jacobs bases her reading on a citation of the Song of Deborah in "*Aesthetica in nuce*," a war hymn featuring two women: the judge Deborah who wakes her people from sleep to wage war[47] and the tent-dwelling desert nomad Jael, who kills Deborah's enemy Sisera by luring him into her tent with a bowl of milk and then hammering a stake through his temple.[48] Hamann's nomads are not nomads in the war machine mode but the transhumant seminomads of the hills and mountains: the herders—shepherds, goatherds, cowherds—living in isolated, elevated zones *within* the geographical bounds of the state. Transhumance is characterized by *migrational repetition*: migrating at various temporal intervals (daily, seasonally, annually) back and forth and up and down between two or three migrational nodes: home, seasonal halfway,[49] and daily pasture. Transhumance, rather than generating lines of flight forever away (which has, of course, as de Quincey's Tartars, the Kalmyks, learned, never been possible, only a point as ideal as Archimedes'), has more the character of weaving:

46    Jacobs, *Skirting the Ethical*, p. 111.
47    "Villagers in Israel would not fight; / they held back until I, Deborah, arose, / until I arose, a mother in Israel" (NIV).
48    "Most blessed of women be Jael, / the wife of Heber the Kenite, / most blessed of tent-dwelling women. / He asked for water, and she gave him milk; / in a bowl fit for nobles she brought him curdled milk. / Her hand reached for the tent peg, / her right hand for the workman's hammer. / She struck Sisera, she crushed his head, / she shattered and pierced his temple" (Judges 5:24–26, NIV).
49    This trilevel kind of transhumance—with its intermediate *Maiensäß*—is still though diminishingly practiced in the Alps, e.g. among the Walsers of Liechtenstein and Vorarlberg, Austria.

the back-and-forth up-and-down solidification of a single spool or skein of thread into textile; the heights of the hills or mountains are not a postulated and subsumed-then-negated transcendent realm above: the above is woven into the below through the rhythmic repetition of migrational weave.

The *skein of immanence*—a single thread "wound and doubled" over and over again, "ravell'd and perplexed," in- and re-folded and compounded and saturated and bundled into solidity—could be a name for a Hamannian counterconcept to Deleuze's *plane of immanence*. This might allow us, with Hamann, to think our way towards a kind of multi-dimensional, elastic solidity to the virtual, a *plasticity of the virtual*. Woven theory is not foldable, creasable paper but a skeining, until the knot or bundle can be held or hold or be beheld.

Pan, god of borderless promiscuous intermingling, of mixture, impromptu, and the delights of the grotesque, was not a god of smooth spaces, of the desert or plains but of caves and mountains and forests: the knot or skein, like a network of caves or forest or labyrinth, has depth and interiority—without transcendence. The skein is an object of folding, infolding, doubling back, density and condensation, bending, tangling, entanglement. Inside the skein, the thread works back in on itself rather than fleeing forever outwards in lines of flight.

The thread remains one-dimensional, in the sense of being a vector or trajectory without thereby becoming a straight line, powered by whatever "energy or enargy [*Enargie*]" (W 306) drives the "single positive force" of panic and desire, the driving force(s) of theory and fiction. The thread also brings *attention* onto the stage, the impossibility of escaping sequence and finding simultaneity.

This dynamics of density, and its theory of *self-actualizing potentia*—irresistible force, power, violence, whatever we want to name it—might have a price, however, as it did for

Hamann like Deleuze after him: exhausted, the thread lost, bewildered by the density and hypersaturation of his own text, he concluded his final handwritten manuscript to Jacobi (R 41), and thus his entire body of work as we have it, with the following words:

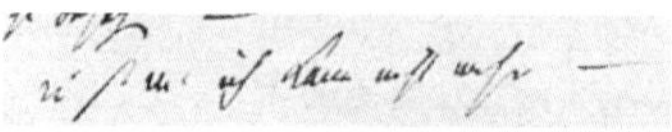

Figure 8: Universitäts- und Landesbibliothek Münster, N. Hamann, 1,49–9.2 (= R 41, 2r).

*usw. ich kann nicht mehr –*

*etc. ich kann nicht mehr*—how should I translate this? I can't anymore, I can do no more, I can't take any more, I have no more to give, it's too much? Or is it Luther's *Hier stehe ich, ich kann nicht anders* at the Diet of Worms lingering in the background, *Here I stand, I can do no otherwise*, I never could have done anything else?

*Mehr* and *anders*, the more and the other—i.e. repetition and difference, quantity and quality: the difference of repetition is one of layering and saturation in sequence like a photocopy of a photocopy of a photocopy, or recording of a recording etc.

To be able to do no otherwise—to have an inevitable and unrepeatable role to play, to be fated—is to have already done the most that one can do: it is the placing of a period, an embrace of the role. The Hamann that thought he could finally remove the final mask and leave his author role behind to stand unclothed, unveiled, and transfigured—exposed, real, actual, a person at last and persona no longer—collided with that other Hamann that knew and repeatedly insisted to others that the loss of a mask is everything else than a gain in reality, in self. This is to be able to do no more and to end with a dash, in et cetera.

Don Quixote, or maybe it was Alfonso Quijada's idea, left his armor hanging on a tree after being challenged and defeated in combat on a beach outside of Barcelona—by an old acquaintance disguised as the Knight of the White Moon (formerly a student disguised as the Knight of the Mirrors) who had been defeated by Don Quixote once before and vowed to take revenge; Don Quesada had drawn him into his role, and had finally found a worthy opponent, worthy to the degree that his opponent took him seriously: it was the first time someone had fought him as an equal, and not as a madman or nuisance or joke or as malicious sport. After a brief, failed attempt to play the new role (from within the old role) of the pastoral shepherd, he and Sancho finally made their way home, where Don Quixote recanted it all to die as Alfonso Quejano.

Hamann never did find his Knight of the White Moon, the friend-become-enemy able to forsake self for role and play the role seriously, first in good humor and then, after the initial defeat, entirely, the role realer now than whatever came before; something I felt uneasily affected by while watching the development of Hamann's correspondence with Jacobi over the last few years of his life (as Jacobi gradually became his almost exclusive correspondent). Hamann's letters begin to stretch over pages and days, get longer and longer, become more of a diary than anything else, a kind of conversation with himself. We see him trying to pretend himself into an accomplished work, making big plans for his now-flying, now-crawling letter, to trick himself or posit himself into getting up from crawling again to fly—while Jacobi's letters become shorter and terser and less frequent, as he, too, finally loses patience and gives himself over to the easier pleasures of his newfound fame. What is left is simply loneliness: Hamann had asked for a Flacius Fulbert and ended up with an F.

He has certainly not found his Knight of the White Moon in me either, as I recognize almost every time I return to the *Letter*, which leaps in every other sentence and every footnote beyond anything I am capable of keeping up with, even with search engines and access to each referenced text; today I noticed a short passage I had simply forgotten about:

> The measure of my "greatness" is that of neither a giant nor an angel, not a hand wider than a common human cubit. That the world not be razed to the ground to clothe and transfigure a rotting sinner in the nimbus of a "saint," please give me no moustaches in my life, as long as I can still laugh along. But I want to take off my own clothes, spread out my hands like a swimmer spreads them out to swim over the still, moving water of oblivion or there to go under.
>
> Do not give my muse cause to worry on her silver anniversary and do not say: But what *is* this garbage? Even this last flirtation is torture. (W 348–349)[50]

Even here, it is all there: the exploitation of grammar in service of exacerbating ambiguity (will the world burn if Hamann

---

50  My translation is less peculiar than the original: "Das Maas meiner 'Größe' sei keines Riesen noch Engels, keine Hand breiter, als eine gemeine Menschenelle. Damit die Welt nicht gebrandschatzt werde, einen verweseten Sünder mit dem Nimbus eines 'Heiligen' zu überkleiden und zu verklären, macht mir lieber keine Schnurrbärte in meinem Leben, so lange ich noch mit lachen kann. Ich will mich aber selbst entkleiden, meine Hände ausbreiten, wie sie ein Schwimmer ausbreitet, um über das stille gehende Wasser der Vergessenheit zu schwimmen oder darinne unterzugehen. / Bekümmert nicht meine Muse bey ihrer silbernen Hochzeitsfeyer und sprecht nicht: was soll doch dieser Unrath? Selbst diese ihre letzte Tandelei ist Tortur."

*is* made a saint, or if he is *not* made a saint?), the manipulation of conjunctions, the collusion of opposites ("still, moving water"), the interjection of the downright peculiar (no moustaches please!), the ambivalent backwards lurch into ancient mysteries (the inversion and embrace of Orphic anti-oblivion) in a doubling (either "swim over" or "go under" in oblivion), etc.

Words become stranger and more foreign in repetition: say *mask* sixty times. That is the immense solitude I eventually encountered in Hamann: where every word feels strange in my mouth.